DIDN'T SEE
THAT
COMING

# DIDN'T SEE THAT COMING

### PUTTING LIFE BACK TOGETHER
### WHEN YOUR WORLD FALLS APART

# RACHEL HOLLIS

**DEY ST.**

*An Imprint of* WILLIAM MORROW

**DEY ST.**

HarperCollins books may be purchased for educational, business, or sales promotional use. For information, please email the Special Markets Department at SPsales@harpercollins.com.

FIRST EDITION

*Designed by Renata De Oliveira*
*Jacket design by Sami Lane*
*Jacket photograph by Vanessa Todd*

Library of Congress Cataloging-in-Publication Data has been applied for.

ISBN 978-0-06-301052-9

20 21 22 23 24  WOR  10 9 8 7 6 5 4 3 2 1

THIS ONE IS FOR RYAN.

# CONTENTS

PROLOGUE  *1*

I CALL BULLSHIT  7

## WHAT TO DO TODAY

*1*  IDENTIFY THE NEW YOU  *29*

*2*  STOP QUESTIONING YOUR SUFFERING  *47*

*3*  LET GO OF GUILT  *67*

## WHAT TO DO TOMORROW

*4*  TRY ON ANOTHER PERSPECTIVE  *81*

*5*  CHANGE YOUR MIND ABOUT GETTING BETTER  *95*

*6*  HACK YOUR COURAGE  *107*

*7*  SHOW UP  *119*

*8*  GET REAL ABOUT YOUR FINANCES  *135*

## WHAT TO DO FOREVER

*9*  BE SURPRISED BY RESILIENCE  *153*

*10*  CLING TO YOUR GOOD HABITS, OR MAKE SOME NEW ONES  *167*

*11*  CHOOSE JOY EVEN WHEN LIFE SUCKS  *181*

*12*  REIMAGINE YOUR FUTURE  *195*

HOLD ON TO HOPE  *209*

ACKNOWLEDGMENTS  *221*

DIDN'T SEE
THAT
COMING

THREE DAYS INTO EDITING THIS BOOK, MY MARRIAGE ENDED.

A sixteen-year marriage to the father of my four children. An eighteen-year relationship with my best friend. The foundation of my life, everything that once was, crumbled between one breath and another.

This book isn't intended as a confessional, as a recounting of the *how* and the *why* this seismic shift in our lives had to happen. I honestly don't know that I'm capable of unpacking that and still staying upright—I'd like to believe that someday I might be strong enough to examine exactly where the fissures took hold, where every small disconnect eroded and made inroads over many years until they cracked us in half, but today is not that day. Like so many couples, we patched over the cracks with kids, with work, with the parts of us that *did* work.

We looked great from the outside because our friendship has always been a tangible thing, even to strangers—but friendship and a romantic relationship are two very different things. Eventually, we became two very different things and that disparity meant that something had to give.

Which is where I find myself today: something had to give.

And it did.

I set out to write this book because I have survived crisis and grief many times and I believed I might have something to share that could help others walk through it. I wrote the first draft as a sort of Sherpa, believing I could help guide you over the mountain of grief. Now I find myself back inside grief and editing from an entirely different perspective than the one from which I wrote. I'm no longer a Sherpa, leading from the front—now I'm also trudging through it with you, which means this book has the unique duality of a creation both outside and inside of pain. As someone who lives by a plan, who has imagined in detail the next two decades of my life and how they might play out, I can honestly tell you, I never planned for *this*. Honestly? The fact that I didn't see this or plan for it makes me feel like an idiot. I will add a bit more honesty to this introduction and tell you something in confidence. I considered pushing this book away or scrapping the idea altogether. I didn't think I was ready—*I wasn't sure I'd ever be ready.* I questioned whether I could teach and learn at the same time—because this lesson, this work, feels like the hardest I've ever done.

Even though the words were written, even though I believed they could be helpful to someone—I knew it was impossible to keep this book in its original form without acknowledging the fresh destruction I find myself in. And the idea of writing about something so new goes against everything I have believed about my work. There's an old expression that says we should teach or write or share only from our *scars,* never from our wounds, and I have lived by it. Meaning, I have been intentional about never processing the hard parts of life *with* you but instead have only ever shared what has been effective for me *after* I've done the work.

But here we are.

Everything feels fragile and scrubbed raw. Everything feels unreal and uncertain. Everything feels absent of all that matters and simultaneously too big to carry.

And so, I sat with it, and prayed and journaled and obsessed and prayed some more. I didn't have the words for anything eloquent and so my prayer became a plea, became the same two words over and over. *Help me.*

These were the only two words I could think.

I was asking for God's help as I moved forward day by day. As I made decisions. As I answered the questions my children asked. As I faced the changes in my work. As I sat with my husband and we talked about the future. As I contemplated how to finish this book. And so much more.

*Help* me. Help *me?* Help me!

I prayed unceasingly and always aloud, falling back on a childhood superstition that if I didn't speak the words out into the ether God might not hear. Those two words became a litany, became lines in a journal, became the last thing I said before falling asleep at night and my first thought upon waking. And somewhere through the darkness of all that was, if not an easing of the pain, at least a seed of clarity.

My work has always been honest. Whether approved of or ridiculed, my books have always been a big offering of my truth in the season they were written. To remove that truth from my work now would be too great a loss in the midst of so many others.

So here we are, you and I, standing in the midst of pain. Some of us are trying to make sense of the scars of our past. Some of us are holding gaping wounds together with hands that tremble and shake. But we're still here. Together.

I believe we are strong enough to do the work of healing, even if at times the effort makes us feel weaker than before we began. Don't fear your own weakness, fear drowning in despair for the rest of your time on earth because you were too afraid to confront your pain. In the following pages I will try my best to do just that. I will examine the pain and break it apart and laugh at it when possible and cry over it when necessary, but I will not— not ever again in my life—cover up my pain to make other people more comfortable.

And neither should you.

This book is my work as much as it is yours. Let's do it together.

## I CALL BULLSHIT

Can we all just take a minute?

Can we just—I mean . . . what in the *actual almighty world* just happened? I mean, I'm assuming you're not just reading this book for the hell of it. I'm assuming you grabbed it (or someone grabbed it for you) because you're feeling like the main event in a butt-kicking contest. I assume you're here because some part of your world (or maybe the whole of it) got turned inside out and you're trying to find your way back. So, before we run into what to do to change anything or help anything, let's take a second and call bullshit.

Seriously.

I know it's not polite. I know it's not what "good girls" do. Good girls don't call bullshit. In fact, good girls don't even know the word *bullshit*. It seems everyone would prefer that when we're hurt or scared or uncertain that we don't bother anyone else with it. Or at least keep our feelings at an "acceptable" level. "Yes, we know your world is burning down around you but do please hold on to the propriety and stoicism of that quintet who continued to play even as the *Titanic* went down."

No. Not here, my friend. This book, this time together, this is our sacred space. This is an opportunity for you to be real and raw and to hold whatever negative emotion you have about whatever you're going through. I won't judge you . . . *I literally can't even see you right now.* We're about to talk about some hard things and every single chapter from here on out is about trying to help you get through the place you're in. But . . . it's going to be impossible to move forward if you can't first acknowledge that it sucks mightily that you're here in the first place. So, can we just say it? Can we just call that thing you went through what it is? Can we just agree that it's unfair or unjust or harsh or just awful? Feel free to use whatever descriptive words you can to call this what it is. Be sure to add in cuss words too if the spirit moves—after all, it's not like anyone can hear your inner thoughts. It's just me, you, and the reality of that thing you went through? It's the fucking worst.

Yep. I said it. Two cuss words in play and it's not even

chapter one. But you know what, so what. Right now, in this exact moment in my life, I'm so sick of the words *I'm sorry* I could punch something. When my brother committed suicide, everyone was sorry. When we lost those twin babies we had loved and hoped to make part of our family, everyone was sorry. When my marriage ended, everyone was sorry. I appreciate the sentiment and the prayers and the well wishes but here's something only people who have gone through hard things understand— other people being sorry only adds to your pain. When people say they're sorry the polite response is "It's okay" or "I'm fine" or some other inane platitude to make the other person feel safe to be around your misery. I'm not okay. I'm ten thousand different emotions, none of which I want to handle in a polite way right now, and I don't think you should either.

So, let's acknowledge that this sucks.

Then, let's go one better. Let's acknowledge how frightening this is and how hard it is and how much we wish it weren't happening—*and* let's allow ourselves to be deeply disappointed by the unfairness of it all. Oh, I'm sure you've had all kinds of feelings about the state that you're in, but when crisis happens the emotions that swirl to the top are big and violent in their consumption of us. *Disappointment* seems a small word and feeling by comparison, but at its core what it means is that someone or something has failed to live up to your hopes or expectations.

Maybe your partner disappointed you. Maybe your child disappointed you. Maybe the economy came crashing down just when you were starting to make strides in your finances, and it's disappointed you. Maybe life disappointed you because what you hoped for and dreamed of feels impossible because of loss. Maybe all of this feels like just another disappointment in a string of many. And maybe, if you can allow yourself to be honest about what it feels like for you, instead of pretending that you're strong enough to ignore the negative emotions, you'll actually be able to overcome them and move forward.

Have you ever covered old paint? I know I'm terrible at transitions, but just go with me for a minute. Imagine that you've just bought a little bungalow in the suburbs of your favorite city. If it's L.A. that bungalow costs you a cool million, if it's Minneapolis you got it for $153,000 using your used Honda Civic as a down payment—either way, imagine that the bathroom in your new little bungalow is a hideously shiny avocado green.

And for clarity, this is not freshly cut avocado green . . . this is that weird poopy green color the avocado turns when it's gotten more than six minutes of access to oxygen. You're so excited about your new home but the poopy green avocado bathroom is the first thing you want to change. You think it'll be easy. You think you just need to pick out a fabulous new color to spread over the top of that offending shade of rotting produce. So, you go get all your supplies and you turn on some music and putrid avocado gives way to the fresh off-white of Swiss Coffee with each glide of your roller brush. You're so proud of yourself. You covered up that offending shade with something that's much more appropriate, much more *you*. Every time you walk by your darling little bathroom the color of a newly laid egg, you feel deeply satisfied with yourself.

A few days later you decide to take a long, hot bubble bath to soak your aching muscles after all the work you've done on the house. You get the water to the perfect bath temperature—hot enough to turn your whole body lobster red—and then you slide down and lie there long enough that your fingers and toes are shriveled until the prints could no longer incriminate you at a crime scene.

As you stand to get out of the tub . . . you gasp in horror when you see it. All around your newly decorated bathroom, that fresh coat of paint is bubbling up. Your walls have the complexion of an eighth grader in the throes of puberty. What on earth? You reach out and touch one of the biggest bubbles and it breaks, revealing the offending avocado it was before. What just happened?

Well, in home remodel terms, what just happened is that you tried to put a fresh coat over an old coat but didn't do anything to make sure the new paint would stick. Also, the original paint was likely a high gloss, making it incredibly difficult to cover. On top of an improper application, you then created a perfect storm for the destruction of your project with both heat and moisture from your bath. Your bathroom makeover never stood a chance.

What does any of this have to do with what you're currently living with? Nothing at all. The paint has nothing at all to do with what you're going through, but it's a perfect illustration for you trying to pretend that you don't have negative, ugly feelings about what's happening when you do. Or even better, maybe you're allowing yourself to process the feelings that are *allowed* and *acceptable* but covering up the ones that might make people think less of you.

If we tiptoe back over to the paint analogy for a second, the right way to have remodeled that bathroom involves both sandpaper and a coat of primer. Said another way, you first have to dig into the offending layer, then you have to add another layer of work to make sure the next layer sticks.

Hello! Is this thing on??

If you want to move forward, be honest about what's going on *even if it's only to yourself.* When the world basically shut down in the spring of 2020 due to the pandemic there was so much disappointment and grief but there was also a weird comparison of misfortune going on that made nearly everyone I know feel like their disappointment was petty and small.

It wasn't small and it wasn't petty. It matters that you're disappointed because *you matter.*

All our poor seniors who lost their last year in college or high school. All those kids who were looking forward to prom or finishing out the basketball season. My fifth grader! My poor fifth grader was so excited to "graduate" fifth grade even though you and I both know fifth grade graduations are lame. Bless his heart. But in quarantine, all the parties and plans or whatever other cool things they do for fifth graders in Texas—those were all gone.

He was sad and just because there were seniors in high school and seniors in college who were also sad for bigger life events, that doesn't take away Sawyer's right to feel disappointed himself.

Then there were all those couples whose weddings had to be canceled or postponed or maybe the wedding still happened, but it was on Zoom. *A ZOOM wedding!!* In the name of all that is holy! You are allowed to be disappointed. You can be excited about your partner and your future and still be bummed as hell that you didn't get the chance to do the sparkler send-off you've been planning for months. Don't come at those sweet disappointed brides! Did you have to get married on a freaking computer? No?! Then shut it!

In the midst of all that, our country saw yet another heinous crime against an unarmed Black man. Folks took to the streets, for all the right reasons, to protest the brutality. To cry out for all the lives that had been taken and for hundreds of years of systematic oppression in our country. It was necessary, and it was powerful. It was also a time for those of us who have not felt the sting of that pain to think long and hard about our actions and words. It was time for change, and the fact that we still need it is the ultimate calling of bullshit. I felt disappointment in my country, in myself, in the fact that hatred still runs so deeply and fear still rules so many people's lives. This was a different kind of disappointment, one I and so many of us felt in our bones.

So . . . I'd like you to save yourself some time. I'd like you to admit to yourself the truth about what you're feeling about whatever you're going through even if the emotions don't feel polite. You are human, you are not perfect, and as far as I know, you're not the Dalai Lama with his infinite wisdom and equanimity. Though if by chance you are the Dalai Lama, *What up, Your Holiness, I'm a big fan! Please consider leaving an online review!*

Stop trying to cover up your emotions, or, frankly, anything you don't like about yourself or your feelings, with a new coat of paint. You want a remodel? You want to build something new of your own design? That is absolutely possible and I'm the biggest believer you'll ever find in your ability to do that. But in order to do that, you've got to be real. You have to allow yourself to truly *feel* what you feel before you can feel what you'd like.

So now that we've acknowledged how we really feel— disappointed, sad, scared, maybe even angry, what can we do? Are we stuck here forever? No. Not stuck, but for a moment, we must be still. When I was younger, I would have done everything in my power to rush by a season as awful as this one. I would have worked too much or drank too much or distracted myself in every way possible rather than acknowledge my pain. But now I know better. Now, I am still. And I allow myself to remember.

Grandpa and I liked our potatoes fried. My big brother Ryan and Grandma? They preferred mashed. We used to bicker over which kind of potatoes were better. The answer is still fried.

I didn't remember that until now.

I love growing things in the dirt and wearing cutoff shorts.

I like walking across the grass in bare feet.

I like a cold glass of sun tea. I like when the ice melts so slowly it turns the cup into variegated shades of brown. I don't mind when things get watered down.

I didn't remember that until now.

I still don't like tuna canned in oil—but I've eaten it twice this week because all your capital-T truths and must-haves were really only ever preferences.

I didn't remember that until now.

It often takes a life-changing crisis to remind us which parts of our life are worth living. I had forgotten so many things in the hectic pace of life and work and being a mama and a wife. I was going a hundred miles an hour because that felt like the speed required to be all things to all people. That felt like the centrifugal force required to hold my world together and then, without permission, it blew itself apart.

I don't do drugs, but *damn* did I wish I was a stoner during March 2020.

I remember one night I was making a frozen lasagna for our kids—the last of a stash we'd acquired before the grocery store ran out of all frozen foods because everyone was panic pandemic buying—and I was eyeing the cheese on the top through the oven window. Anyone who's ever used the broil setting to blister their mozzarella knows that you can't look away for even a second because that's the exact moment when broil will smite your dinner. I stared it down through the looking glass for several minutes, and between one blink and another my eyes readjusted, coming into focus on my close-up reflection in the glass. There were my sparsely populated eyebrows—sisters, but never twins, no matter how hard I worked to shape them in my thirty-seven years. There was the beauty mark above my lips—I wondered if the term *beauty mark* translates into other languages or if this facial mole with an inflated sense of self is something unique to the English language. Finally, I peered into my own eyes. I thought about how people say you can see someone's story there, the window to the soul and all that. I wondered what was visible in my eyes. I tried to look at them as an objective third party.

What is the story in these eyes?

If my eyes could talk, what would they say about this circumstance I found myself in? It wasn't hard to see the message in my eyes—for all the strength and fortitude and positivity I fight for every day in my life and work, my eyes held a very different attitude.

*This shit again?*

That's what my eyes were saying. My eyes looked world-weary and exhausted. My eyes looked sad. My eyes looked too tired to feel angry—my eyes have seen a thousand awful things in their thirty-seven years that let them know anger would be wasted in these circumstances. *We've been here before,* my eyes told me, *and we know it's going to suck. I'm worried for my parents and my grandma and for my world. How are we going to get through this?*

I wish I wasn't such an expert on living through things that terrify me. I wish I didn't know so much about surviving trauma. I wish I didn't feel like an authority on being strong for others while the world is falling down around us. There's an old saying the patriarchs in my family used to throw out for just such a train of thought. *You can wish in one hand and crap in the other . . . see which one fills up first.*

So, there I was watching the cheese bubble up like a Stouffer's commercial with one thought swirling around in my head . . . *here we go again.*

And yes, in my weaker moments, I did wish I could be a hippie living somewhere on a commune wearing maxi dresses and never brushing my hair and smoking so much reefer that I didn't worry about what would happen to our friends and families and how much this would devastate our hospitals and our economy. In my more desperate moments I wished for escape.

But because I've been through this weird limbo before, because I'm familiar with terror, because I have walked again and again through pain and I am still here to write this down for you, I can also find peace in the storm. March 2020 and every unsettling week thereafter *did not* shake me loose from my mooring. Instead, I allowed the pressure of it all to anchor me more firmly into the earth. And even later, when the word *divorce* was finally said, when it dropped into our life like a grenade and everything exploded around us, I remained standing in the midst of the fire—consciously clutching the pin, choosing to let it burn rather than remain inside of something that was killing us both.

In times of chaos there isn't room to wonder or worry about what comes next—what comes next doesn't matter. When you're trying to survive this moment in your life, anything longer than today seems impossible. And so, I don't even try.

I've been here before, in this suspended reality. Only this time I choose to exist here without the fear that I will lose myself in the grief. I know we'll get through it—that's one of the most difficult parts about being a survivor. You understand that this will be just another hardship to add to many others. You understand that just because you'll keep waking up each morning doesn't mean that it won't cost you something to keep going.

That's the story my eyes were telling that day.

They knew that we'd all be just fine, but the history living in those eyes understood that being fine in the end would take a tremendous effort in the present. At times I sit with the pain because there is power in accepting the waves of grief. At times I fight back negative emotions when they bubble up with the absolute truth that they won't serve me. But mostly, *mostly* I have stayed present in my body, in my feelings, in my strength, and I have remembered which parts of my life are worth living.

So, I learned to walk barefoot again. I baked a chocolate cake and licked the icing off the mixer attachments and never one time worried about the calories. I remembered things . . . good things I used to love. I remembered the hard things from the past too. I remembered them all and I remembered what is true. I thought long and hard about what I'd want to tell you, as you navigate your own awful, hard times. This book, written during a dark time, is a collection of those things I'd have you know.

I want you to know that what's been good will always be good: the smell of coconut sunblock, a five-year-old showing you the spot where his front tooth used to be, a home-cooked meal, when your love kisses that *exact* spot on your neck, a grandmother's handwriting, a job well done, the kindness of strangers, the human spirit, an Appaloosa horse, the ritual of your faith, laughing until you pee your pants a little, holiday dessert tables, first birthday parties, a perfect cup of coffee with a view. What's good will always be good, and one of the most awful, beautiful things about the hard seasons is that unless we experience hardship, we'll never truly appreciate and remember the good that was always good.

You don't need a catastrophic event to appreciate the good things in your life—but my gut says that if you picked up this book there's a solid chance you've gone through (or are going through) one. What I want you to hear me say right here up front is, I get it. I'd like to look you in the eyes and tell you that you're strong enough to survive this—even on the days that feels impossible. You are strong enough and *it is* possible to come out the other side as a better version of yourself.

Yes, I said *better.*

You must decide *right now* that while your hardship will beat you up and it may rob you of whole pieces, you will not lose yourself in the grief. It is possible to glean lasting, positive change from even the most terrible situations.

I've watched people go through awful divorces and come out the other side as more compassionate, more present parents than they ever were when they were still married. I've witnessed women, once victims of domestic violence themselves, go on to build nonprofit organizations that would save thousands of others who were once in their shoes.

You *can* come through your pain as someone better than you went into it.

When humans go through something hard, they react in one of two ways. They come out the other side either better or worse. It's impossible to walk through hell and leave it the same way you went in. Nobody walks through fire unscathed. You either burn up into ashes or you get forged in the flames and emerge as something new.

So, what will you choose?

Will you allow this season that you're in to wear you down and diminish you? Will you become bitter or angry? Will you live the rest of your life drowning in anxiety and fear of being hurt again? Will you allow loss to define you for the rest of your life? Or will you fight back?

Because make no mistake, *this will be a fight*. Finding your center again, reaching for joy, honing your strength, claiming your faith, having the courage to move forward when you've been battered and bruised? Those things will take every ounce of your ability and none of them is achieved quickly. It won't be easy, *but it is possible.*

I'm going to fill the pages of this book with everything I can think of that helped me through the most difficult seasons of my past—and what I am leaning on today as I navigate a new one. Grief, loss, anger, hurt, abandonment, fear, desperation—I am intimate with them all. Writing about them now isn't an attempt to elicit sympathy or gain significance from what I've been through. I actually—honestly—never meant to make the worst parts of my story anecdotes for millions of strangers. I've written about these hard things in my other books for two reasons. One, because I want you to know that nothing I'm sharing is "expert" information or something I learned through the study of other people's pain and hardship. The things I share and the lessons I teach are all built around one thing: what helped me. I share it hoping that it will be helpful for you too and if it's not, then at the very least you've read about the journey I went on to find my way out of the woods and perhaps that will spark something that encourages you to forge your own path. The second reason I share these stories is because *I want them to have meant something.* All the pain, all the hardship, I want it to have been for more than just that I was dealt a shitty hand. I believe it's possible to find meaning in anything; I believe how I deal with the hard parts of my past and how I manage them in the present is me taking back ownership. I cannot control what happened to me in the past or what I must endure in the present but I for damn sure get to choose how I respond to both. I choose to fight for a better life. I think you're here because you have a warrior spirit as well and you want to stand back up and go again.

I'm glad you're here.

I'm proud of you saying what you need.

Let's get to work.

WHAT TO DO
TODAY

# 1

## IDENTIFY THE NEW YOU

I think one of the hardest things about going through a world-rocking, life-changing experience is that you come out the other side as someone totally different, only your mind is still processing what's happened as *who you were* not as *who you are now*. It's like one of those sci-fi movies when the spaceship moves into hyperdrive or warp speed or whatever they call it and then the galaxies all blur into streaks and suddenly the *Enterprise* is in another dimension. You have become something else. You've moved on to an entirely new dimension but your sense of self—the you that makes up your thoughts and feelings—is still the you who you always *were*.

Life is so rude sometimes.

As if it weren't enough that you've got to deal with the emotional upheaval of what you're experiencing, now you also have to contend with a big old identity crisis. Only most of us won't see the crux of the problem as a question of identity, which makes it harder still.

In my opinion, there are four different kinds of identity crisis as it pertains to loss/pain/grief:

1. **YOU HAD AN IDENTITY AND IT WAS TAKEN AWAY FROM YOU**—"I was a great worker, but my company laid me off. Now I'm just unemployed."

2. **YOU WANT AN IDENTITY THAT IS DENIED TO YOU**—"I wanted to be a mom so badly, but the IVF treatment didn't work and I'm devastated."

3. **YOU CHOSE AN IDENTITY AND NO LONGER WANT IT**—"I thought that I was happy as a stay-at-home mom, but actually, I'm depressed and not a good mama to my kids."

4. **SOMEONE ELSE CHOSE AN IDENTITY FOR YOU THAT ISN'T WHO YOU ARE**—"Being in this management role keeps me from being creative, but my boss thinks I'm needed here. I feel like I'm dying inside."

For a more visual illustration, let me try using a subject I know almost nothing about, basketball.

Let's begin with the first one, *the identity you had was taken away from you*. Several years back I was speaking at an event for the Navy SEAL Foundation and I had the honor of meeting with a smaller community of Gold Star Families. If you're not familiar, Gold Star Families are those that have lost a loved one in military service, and that day there were about fifty women who had lost their SEAL in service. I have worked with the military a lot over the years—it's a community that is incredibly close to my heart and a big focus of the philanthropy we do through our foundation. That's why I know I'll offend some of them when I say this, because all branches of military service are incredible and inspiring and so proud—but nobody, and I mean *nobody,* has a stronger sense of military pride and identity than the Navy SEALs. I think that's why this memory is so vivid, because while I've yet to meet a military spouse who wasn't proud of their service member, the SEAL wives are a breed unto themselves. As I sat in the room that day, I heard stories of loss from decades before and others from just a few months prior but the narrative I heard again and again was . . . "I was *his* wife, and now he's gone. Who am I now?"

*Who am I now?* I've heard that line from mothers who have lost their only child and men who have lost their jobs. I've heard it from athletes who've had a career-ending injury and college students who've been dumped. When I think of this identity crisis in terms of basketball, it's akin to having your series-winning shot blocked. Have you ever seen a game where an incredible player takes the game-winning shot that is for sure, absolutely going in and at the last second, without warning, it's violently batted away by someone on the other team? The pain of that is all the more intensified by the fact that you *just had it* . . . it was just here . . . and now suddenly it's been ripped away from you.

I can't begin to tell you why this has happened to you but when it comes to your identity on this particular point, I need you to hear me. You are still his wife. You are still her mama. You are still an incredible asset to a team. You are still an amazing athlete. You are still a great boyfriend. Just because the thing attached to that identity was removed doesn't mean that the **role you earned** was taken away. Nobody can remove your identity from you. You are a great and loving partner, even if your boyfriend broke up with you. Just because he's too much of a jackass to know how special you are doesn't make you any less wonderful. Don't you see? Identity literally means being who or what you are. And *you* get to choose that.

That day with the Gold Star Families, each and every woman's story vacillated from sadness to rage depending on who was speaking. I do not know much about the people in that room beyond the time that I spent with them, but I can tell you one thing for sure, they were warriors on par with the men they had lost. They were so strong and even in their pain and their grief they would keep going. The Navy SEALs have a creed and one line in particular always reminds me of the women in the room that day: *"If knocked down, I will get back up, every time."*

I'm writing it for you now, so you can memorize it. **If you've had something ripped away, if you've been knocked down, get back up. Every time.** Wear the identity you earned with pride.

The second kind of identity crisis is the opposite of the first . . . *You want an identity that is denied to you.* If the first one is to have your shot blocked, then the basketball equivalent for this one would be calling your shot and having it bounce off the rim, no matter how hard you try.

To take another approach, let's try this.

When I was a little girl, I wanted to be a zoologist.

Our local library was giving away old magazines and since I'd never had a magazine to call my very own, I leapt at the chance to take a stack that ran the gamut from *National Geographic* to *Mad* magazine. Somewhere in that stack, one such magazine had a story of a zoo—which zoo? I don't remember. What was the article about? I can't recall. What I *do* know for sure is that the featured image of this article was a sick baby orangutan being held lovingly in the arms of a zookeeper who was nursing it back to health. A sick, slightly bald baby monkey with little wisps of hair and a diaper that would fit a four-month-old human. Just imagine.

I looked into the sad eyes of that sweet baby monkey and made a decision then and there . . . I would be a zoologist and I would hold baby monkeys and I would nurse them back to health and teach them sign language and give zoo tours to fourth graders on their class field trip. By God, I had a plan! I tore out the page and taped it to my wall, where it would reside for *years*. My future was clear and I knew who and what I was going to become. Only, here's the thing . . . I don't like to get dirty, and I definitely don't like animal fur and I for sure don't like animal poop or getting hot and dusty, or smelling like creatures, or ruining my manicure . . . I mean. My friends will tell you that there isn't a job I'm less suited for than zookeeper. I spent many years of my life thinking I would be that one thing but of course as a little girl, I didn't know myself well enough to make a lifelong decision about who I would become. There was no real harm done—after all, the identity I'd claimed for myself was my adorable childhood fantasy.

But what if the identity you've claimed for yourself isn't just a childhood dream? What if it's a very real, grown-up vision and the crisis or trauma you find yourself inside of is that no matter how much you want it or how hard you've prayed, hoped, and worked, that identity doesn't come to fruition? How many women have hoped every month of the last year would be *the* month— that this time they'll find out they're pregnant—only to discover that they're unable to become a mother in the way they'd imagined? They had a clear vision of who they were—they only needed the evidence of the identity they'd known in their heart and it can be a soul-shredding disappointment when it doesn't happen. If you find yourself in that kind of identity crisis, I don't for one second think you should give up on your dream. Fight for it. Find a way . . . you may just need to adjust *how* you're going to make that dream become a reality. Focus on the destination you want to head toward but be open to the route you take to get there. I truly believe it's possible to achieve anything you want, with hard work, but you don't get to control the variables that will make it so or the time frame in which it appears.

The third identity crisis is one that many people find themselves in, particularly as they begin to evolve . . . *you chose an identity for yourself that you no longer want.* Or, in basketball terms again, you're wearing a uniform that no longer fits. This can feel truly uncomfortable, both physically and spiritually.

I am personally intimate with this particular crisis as I lived through it several years ago. I was a mother of two young sons, a wife and a small-business owner, and I was deeply unhappy. The problem wasn't the life I had chosen. The problem was that I realized I was made for more than just the life I had chosen but I also understood that the people around me wouldn't like for me to change. My "uniform," the one I'd worked hard for and was proud to wear, no longer fit me but I was too afraid to say anything. Instead I lived with debilitating anxiety and played the role that made everyone else feel most comfortable even though I was miserable. I wrote a whole book about this topic called *Girl, Stop Apologizing* if you want to take a deeper dive in, but I want to tell you two things about it really quick. The first is that people don't often realize they're having this crisis of self; in my experience it usually shows up as anxiety brought on by a desire to people please. This person knows, even subconsciously, that this identity is no longer who they really are, but they also don't want to upset anyone by speaking their truth. Instead they try to gain a sense of purpose through other people's approval rather than their own freedom of self. The other thing you need to know about the fear you have of exchanging your jersey can be summed up with another sports analogy. All great players are continually working to become better—why would you be any different? Of course you're different from the woman he married . . . that was fourteen years ago! Of course you're not the same little brother they're used to . . . who on earth is the same person at twenty-six as they were at sixteen? The greatest sports stars on earth, the ones we love and admire, they didn't peak in the beginning. The greatest kept getting better, they kept leveling up. If someone tries to make you feel badly with the line "You've changed" your only response should be *Thank you, I'm working at it!* Trust me, the grief and the pain that come from staying put in order to keep those around you comfortable are not an indication of a life well lived. For them, or you.

The last identity crisis is when someone else *chooses an identity for you that you never agreed to take on.* In sports terms, imagine that you became a basketball player because it was your father's dream. You never even had the chance to consider something else because you were swept up in his vision for you, and since he is such an important person in your life, it felt impossible to get out from under it. To explain this one fully I have to first tell you a little bit about my own identity—at least as it pertains to, well, you. Or maybe not *you* exactly but a specific group of people who know as much about me as they know about their own sister . . . but whom I don't know anything about at all. These people are strangers to me but to them, I'm someone they know well. This identity was not something I chose for myself nor is it one I've been familiar with for very long. To be specific, it's been around for almost exactly two years. Why do I know the exact timing of this anomaly? Because it began happening just about six months after my first nonfiction book came out. Because that particular book was what made most people aware of me, their awareness had very little to do with my own personal identity but was instead shaped by the identity created for me by their having read that book. I had a small social media following at the time so I'd gotten used to an occasional request for a selfie but then almost overnight that rarity turned into strangers walking up to me in public and promptly bursting into tears as they told me about their childhood trauma or their cheating boyfriend or the grief they couldn't let go of. The first time it happened to me at a book signing it was startling. When it began happening at airports, several times in every city, it made me nervous. When a woman at my local grocery store didn't even say hello before she started crying and telling me about her sexual abuse as a teenager—all while my six-year-old son held my hand and nervously looked up at me to explain what was happening—when *that* happened, it fully sent me into months of the kind of anxiety attacks I hadn't had in years. This new level of notoriety was already something difficult to navigate—but because nearly every interaction came with so much emotion and trauma to carry, I had no idea how to manage it. I understood why women were telling me these stories . . . I had shared my own hard truths and so I knew they wanted solidarity and, in many cases, had never told anyone what they'd gone through. I was, and am, deeply humbled that people trust me with their stories. But it's not something anyone is prepared to handle in a Target aisle when buying school supplies and I had no idea how to manage it. I never knew when someone might show up unexpectedly and if they did, I didn't know if I should brace myself to hear something hard or console them while they cried. I held tightly to the belief that *to whom much is given, much is expected* . . . I kept thinking that this new aspect of my life must be part of God's plan. Clearly this was a role I was meant to play even if I didn't quite know how. I was so terrified of offending a reader or not being present to receive whatever someone wanted to tell me that I was totally open. I started to receive thousands and thousands of DM's every day, and I spent hours trying to respond to as many as I could.

I became almost agoraphobic in my fear of leaving my house. I never knew if it was safe to go out in public. Home was the only place I felt secure—felt free to be myself, just Rach to my closest friends, just Mom to my kids, just Rae to my husband. Home was the sacred place . . . and then my address found its way onto the Internet. Or should I say that the Internet found its way to my address? Either way, packages and letters and gifts started to arrive in droves. People began dropping things in our mailbox or showing up in my neighborhood while

I was on a run to ask advice. They started showing up at church on Sunday. They started finding me at the gym before the sun came up.

I'll be honest. It was terrifying for me.

Each and every time someone came up to talk about hard things, I spoke with them about it and did my best to offer advice or love on them the best that I could. When the letters came in the mail I opened every single one because—and I'll be completely transparent—in the anxious state that I was living in, I felt like I had to play this role that others needed from me and I was terrified that someone would reach out and tell me they were suicidal (something that is obviously incredibly triggering to me) and that I wouldn't be there when they needed me because I hadn't opened their letter. I spent half a year in this unending cycle and in the midst of it all the success of the book and the attention it garnered suddenly shifted—it was no longer about the people who liked my work, now the book's success was fodder for people who didn't. First it was blog posts and then long diatribes in the press all pointing to the reasons I was a terrible influence for women or a bad Christian . . . more identities that other people gave me and since I had dissolved all of my boundaries at that point, I believed those must be true for me as well.

It's a strange phenomenon I've noticed about my work—and frankly, that of other female creators regardless of what they create: When people don't like a book written by a man, they say the book is bad. When they don't like something created by a woman, they say *she is bad*.

I digress.

It took me about nine months of soul searching and prayer and, yes, more therapy to begin to understand that just because I had been given this identity by people I care about, that didn't mean that I had to live into who *other people* wanted or needed me to be. It took me nearly a year to understand how to do this work with you, my community, while also retaining the boundaries that allow me to be who I truly am: Mama and Rae and Rach. I am positive that as long as I live I'll continue to navigate the identities that other people have for me, but the simple act of understanding that I'm not required to take on a label just because someone wants me to is truly the only way I'm able to live authentically as myself.

Please know that I am grateful to all my readers and followers and fans in more ways than I can even describe. Admitting that some parts of that relationship haven't been healthy for me was not easy, but it felt necessary because my gut says that you may have your own version of that experience even if it didn't play out in the same way. What identities are you carrying because you care so much about the people who gave them to you? What are the areas in your life where you've dissolved boundaries to be present for others at the loss of yourself? I know it is possible for me to do this work, and to show up well for my community while being true to myself. I believe it's possible for you too, but first you must decide which identity you will choose going forward.

Identity is who you are, and the most important lesson I want you to take away from this chapter is that you are so much more than the trauma you are living in, whatever that looks like. Your identity is just that, yours. You might have cancer, but you are more than a cancer patient. He might think of you just as a middle manager, but if your identity is a creative powerhouse, live into that! If you feel trapped by your identity because you know it is hurting you, break free and do the work to claim the truth that fits you now. No one gets to define you but you.

## THINGS THAT HELPED ME

**SPEAK YOUR TRUTH, EVERY DAY:** Have the courage to admit who you are, even if it's only to yourself at first. When I have claimed a new identity for myself, I have always worn something daily as a reminder of my truth. For instance, when I wanted so desperately to be a published author, I wore a little cheap bracelet on my wrist stamped with the word count of my manuscript. It was a reminder to myself that I had accomplished a major goal (writing all those words) and that I could accomplish another one (having those words bound in a book). Nobody else knew what my bracelet meant but every day I looked down and saw it, it was a reminder of who I believed myself to be.

**CREATE BOUNDARIES FOR YOURSELF:** Recently I asked my therapist how I should know where or when I needed a boundary. She told me that whenever someone in my life consistently did something that upset me but I didn't comment on it because I thought I was being selfish to admit that it was hurting me, *that* was where I needed a boundary.

This is sort of revolutionary for me because I have been made to believe that there is no greater negative attribute than being selfish. In the past I have done things that slowly destroyed me rather than risking upsetting others but I now understand that we are allowed to state what we need without shame and without holding the recrimination of others. Remember, you are who you want to be. You're in charge. This means that it is okay to say no to people who ask things of you that you do not feel equipped to give. If you need space to be you, or if the role you're being asked to play is uncomfortable, don't be afraid to draw those lines for your own good.

*ACKNOWLEDGE THAT IDENTITIES EVOLVE:* We can and do change. Sometimes because something life-shattering happens, and sometimes because we've outgrown the identity we started with. Evolution is uncomfortable but that doesn't mean it's bad. Try viewing this as a positive movement forward in your life.

## 2

We have to talk about feelings of suffering, because this is a book many of you picked up because you are suffering. You're in the middle of pain or loss. You're encountering any combination of anxiety, fear, depression, rage, bitterness, loss of self, and more. Maybe you've been living with those feelings for so long it feels more normal for you to exist in that state than it does to know any other reality. When my brother died, I heard about the "stages of grief" for the first time. Psychiatrist Elisabeth Kübler-Ross coined the term back in the sixties and the model is still used today. It's a cycle that most people go through while they experience grief and it usually unfolds like this: denial, anger, depression, bargaining, acceptance.

I remember hearing about it as a fourteen-year-old and wondering when we'd get to the acceptance stage. It felt like my whole family had been living in the worst parts of that cycle for months and months and I just wanted a reprieve. I certainly felt the emotions Dr. Kübler-Ross taught about, but for me, my suffering followed an entirely different track.

I wonder if it's the same for you.

I didn't struggle as much with the big abstract feelings Kübler-Ross named in the grief cycle. Those seemed more like statements of fact that I couldn't get out from under. Grief just *is*. Anger *is*. In seasons of immense loss, they are as real and true as a physical presence beside you in the room. Because they're known, they're expected and therefore *accepted* as part of the journey. If something is known, then at the very least you can talk about it or process what you're feeling. But the worst of our suffering often hides inside the things we don't know how to verbalize or are too afraid to share. For me, that looked like questions. The endless rounds of questions that my mind would ask me all day, *every day*. These were queries I had no answers for. These were questions that only begat more questions and with every new layer I uncovered, my anxiety and fear would rise. These questions have showed up for me so often in times of hardship that I've learned to spot the scenarios that will trigger them now.

**I'D LIKE TO WALK YOU THROUGH HOW THEY SHOW UP FOR ME.** I think of my suffering questions in terms of The Five W's. Remember in school when we learned about *Who, What, When, Where,* and *Why*? Well, for me, those questions are what were triggered during my suffering. They're incredibly dangerous to my peace of mind during a hardship or crisis.

# WHO

This one is perhaps the most obvious of the list as I'm sure you can understand that when we experience loss, pain, or trauma it's easy to obsess over the person or people who are part of that pain with us. "*Who*" is a fairly straightforward question but depending on the circumstances "*who*" can cause you different types of pain for different reasons.

> **WHO (TRIGGERED BY LOSS)**—I sort of wish this is the one I struggled with the most when my brother Ryan died. While mourning was painful, I think it would have been more peaceful to just mourn

the loss of my sibling rather than what I did obsess over. More on that in a moment. With this question the thing causing you the most suffering is the loss of the person themselves. You are hyperfocused on their absence. The only thing you can see is what's missing and this becomes the lens through which you view your entire world. The holidays are no longer Thanksgiving or Christmas—now they're "our first Thanksgiving without Papa" or "Christmas was the last time I saw Mom before she passed away." If you're trapped inside this particular obsession it colors everything. Any moment of happiness is touched by the sadness or guilt of who is missing. The thing I can tell you is that focusing on the person you lost is totally normal—to an extent. It is normal to miss your loved ones or to miss the role that someone played in your life. I will miss my brother until the day I leave this earth and I'm positive in the time that I have left here— however long that may be—I will miss others who pass on as well. The difference is, I don't obsess over his loss now the way I did when he died. I'm able to mourn him and the incredible role he played in my life, but I don't allow his absence to affect everything else. I bring this up because I'm positive there are people reading this who are still grieving so heavily that their loss is causing them to lose again and again. Their grief over death is making them miss the life that's still here. I can't tell you how to grieve, that is an incredibly personal process that nobody is in charge of but you. But I can tell you something with absolute certainty: the person you lost would not want this for you. The person you lost would never, ever want you to suffer over their absence. If anything, they'd want you to experience the bittersweet memories of your time together. They'd want you to be happy, they'd want you to laugh again, they'd want you to live the fullest, richest life you can. They'd never choose for you to be anchored to their death by your grief. If this is something you're struggling with then ask your heart what is true. Pretend that your loved one is standing with you now and ask them what they'd want for your life. It's okay to be sad. It's okay to miss them. It's *not* okay for you to lie down and die too. You are still here and there's a reason for that! The greatest thing you can do to honor the memory of whom you lost is to continue to live the life they cannot.

*WHO (TRIGGERED BY HURT)*—Not all suffering because
of another person comes from loss; just as often,
it comes from pain. In this instance the *who* is
focused on the person who hurt you. Being hurt by
another can take on thousands of different forms.
A partner who cheated. A parent who left. A family
member who abused. A friend who took advantage.
It shows up in different ways for all of us but when
we focus only on this *who,* the effects can be lasting
and devastating. For me, I've found that whenever
I focus on the "perpetrator" it's typically because on
some unconscious level I'm trying to protect myself.
My subconscious seems to believe that if I can just
identify every single thing about this person and
their motives then I can keep myself from being
hurt again. The problem with this approach is that
we begin to see those motives in others whether or
not they're actually there. We obsess so much over
the "bad guy" we begin to see everyone around us as
a bad guy too. In some instances, we begin to blame
the other person for not just the major harm they
did us but other negative things that might happen.
That "*who*" becomes the cause of many of our
problems in one way or another and this attitude

invariably begins to erode the ownership we have of our own life. I could probably write an entire book just on this issue alone but let me summarize what I want you to hear with this: Obsessing over this person and why they did what they did will not serve you. You are not defined by the pain they inflicted—***you are defined by what you turn that pain into.*** Will you allow it to make you bitter? Will you allow it to erode your joy? Will you allow that person to keep you from living your life—the only single chance you'll ever have to do so? I hope not. You have so very much to offer this world and try as they might, that person can't stop you from shining your light for all the world to see.

# WHAT

The next kind of suffering comes from an obsession over *what* happened. What exactly happened? This is what I found myself focusing on in a recurring loop when my brother died. If you're like I was during that time, you go over every single detail of what occurred leading up to, during, and after the thing that caused you pain. I always believed that my mind did this because it was trying to process (whether I wanted it to or not) the horrific things I'd seen the day he died. But I also think in other situations, there's shame wrapped up in this process too. Combing through those details again and again is your subconscious asking over and over, *What did I miss? What signs were there? What kept me away that day? What didn't I know?* Of these four questions, there are likely some that make you spiral more than others. Those are the ones for which there simply aren't answers. For those questions about what you missed, what signs you should have seen, the truth is, you aren't all-knowing. You can think about what happened from every angle, but it won't unmake the past. It won't bring someone back. It won't undo the hurt. What it will cause you is more and more depression about who or what was lost or anxiety about an uncertain future.

# WHEN

As in, *When is this going to be over? When will this pain stop? When will I stop crying every day? When will people stop asking me if I'm okay?* When you lament about "*when*" with these questions, what you're really, truly asking is *When will my life go back to normal? When will it be like it was?* I'm sorry that you have to hear this, but I love you enough to tell you the truth—your life will **never** go back to the way it was. Whatever it is you've lived through has changed you. Whether it's changed you for the better or worse is something only you can decide. There is no way you'll ever unsee what you've seen or unknow what you know. When one thing changes, everything changes, even if it takes you a bit to admit it and adjust.

Life won't ever be the same because *you* won't ever be the same. You're different now and so the world looks different too. It's awful to go through a forced metamorphosis but it truly is possible to find something beautiful in your new reality—unless you keep pining for something that won't ever exist again. Clinging to your past, hoping for a *when* that isn't ever coming, will only keep you from having strength in your present.

# WHERE

*Where,* by definition, pertains to a location—but in this instance, I think of it more as theoretical geography. Suffering over *where* is worrying primarily where you'll be when you've weathered your hard season. *What if I can't get over these feelings and I'm not able to find a job? If I can't find a job, where will I live? How will I pay my bills?*

*What about my family? If I'm not strong, where does that leave them?* This one can spin out into a thousand anxious thoughts, each more terrifying than the rest. When you're in the midst of a crisis, in the heart of the storm, the only thing you can and should focus on is your present. Focus on the day you're in. If this day feels too big, focus on the *next hour* and how to care for yourself for those sixty minutes inside of it. Once you gain strength in your present, then you will find the space and energy you need to dream about the future. Only at that point will you be able to set goals to move forward—because otherwise the anxiety of the unknown will always paralyze you.

# WHY

I don't know a single person who has ever gone through something hard who hasn't been consumed by this question at one point in their journey. *Why? Why did this happen to me? Why did we lose Mama so soon? Why our family? Why my job? Why my child?* We want an answer so desperately because on some level we believe that the answer will make us feel better. Hear me, it won't. If you actually knew that there was a reason you'd been singled out for what you've gone through it wouldn't make you feel better! It would likely make you feel worse. It would likely make you feel terrible, like you'd done something to bring that misfortune or tragedy or pain upon yourself. Or make you feel like life is just unfair and unjust, or that you committed some heinous act for which you were being punished.

Life doesn't work that way. What happened to you didn't happen to you because of something you did wrong. It wasn't something you deserved. It wasn't something you failed at. It wasn't fair because as much as I hate this truth, life isn't fair. There is no rationale for why it happened the way it did even though your mind will try and try to convince you of the opposite in a million different ways. You will not ever find the answer to *why,* so stop looking. Focus instead on what might be gained from all your pain.

# FINALLY . . . HOW?

When you learn the "Five W's" in school as a way to organize your thoughts when writing, there is often a sixth consonant tacked on to the end of that list—"One H" that stands for *How.* These question words also come into play when talking about the basics of journalism—every good news story is supposed to answer these fundamental questions, right? We just went through the *Who, What, When, Where,* and *Why* of suffering, and the fundamental truth that for most of these questions, there just aren't answers. But when it comes to *How,* I want you to know that there is an answer, but this isn't a one-size-fits-all proposition. The *how* here pertains to how you start to move forward, how you start to heal, and how to identify the positive parts of the pain you've experienced. *How* here is up to you, because healing is a solo mission, my friends. You can have—and will need—assists, but the work of this is yours, and the path you take is yours to choose. Let me tell you a story to explain myself here.

The first time I ever went to a personal development conference I invited my team at my company to come with me. The five of us spent four days learning and growing and having our lives changed. I drove everyone the five hours there and back in my minivan—because we are suave like that—and on the way home we were all so excited about our future best selves we could hardly sit still. At some point over the many hours in the car we decided that we needed something that would help us stay in the zone that we'd just gotten into. I'm sure many ideas were thrown out but the one we all agreed on (don't ask me why) was that we would all do a juice cleanse. For clarity, the conference we'd gone to had nothing to do with health *or* juice but a juice cleanse seemed extreme and like something a better version of our selves might do and so we all agreed.

When I got back home, I immediately researched how to do one. Because I lived in L.A. at the time, a land teeming with extreme dieting, there were countless establishments that would help me with my mission. I promptly drove down to a fancy hipster juice place and got the starter pack. If you've never had the pleasure of doing a juice cleanse, let me tell you that it's, frankly, a nightmare. You're so hungry you want to die. You're so hungry you begin to obsess over your next juice—even though it's three hours away and made of, like, beetroot and seaweed. As I recall we were allowed to have one solid "meal" a day, but it could only be leafy greens.

Who designed this plan for us? Satan, I'm sure.

It was a terrible ordeal, but we were all supremely proud of ourselves for making it through those first torturous days. On the morning of my third day of the cleanse I sat at my kitchen counter working. It was early morning, and nobody was awake. I was nursing a cup of hot water with lemon when the only thing I wanted in my life was coffee. And, well, I'm just gonna say it, I was gassy. Going on a juice cleanse causes all sorts of exciting things to happen in your intestines and gas is only one of them. It was still dark out, I was alone, and, well . . . I decided to let that gas out of my body. No one was around to be disturbed by it and it was certainly disturbing me as it danced along my colon so I decided to get rid of it. I pushed a little. I pushed with the same energy as I would lightly tap on my car horn to let the truck in front of me know the light had turned green. Not enough for anything offensive, just enough for a little *toot toot*.

Nothing happened.

I'm embarrassed to say it—I'd honestly prefer that you all believe I don't actually pass gas—but when nothing happened, I did *the lean*. You know what I'm talking about, right? When you're concerned that your gas might be trapped inside your butt cheeks because the way you're sitting is holding them together in a vise death grip? And then you lean over to one cheek to alleviate the butt cheek seal and then you push again?

*That* lean. I did that lean. And I pushed again . . . and promptly shot diarrhea out of my body like a heat-seeking missile.

I was so shocked I couldn't consciously understand

what had just occurred. I was a woman *in my thirties* and I had just pooped my pants at the kitchen counter. Aggressively.

I told this story onstage recently to make our conference audience laugh, and backstage, more than one of those employees who had joined me on that juice cleanse from hell told me the same thing had happened to them—in one form or another—only they never wanted to admit it. We don't recommend juice cleanses—or at the very least, not whatever gas-causing, roughage-based, leafy green one we were trying!

Besides the whole pooping-my-pants episode, what I do remember about that time is one of the people with me on that trip was my best friend Sami—who is married to my other best friend Beans—and when Sami came home all fired up with guns blazing and energy high and spouting to Beans about everything she'd just been through, Beans was confused. When Sami announced, "And we're going on a juice cleanse and you should do it too, it will be so great!" Beans, very wisely, responded, "Babe, I didn't have your experience, I didn't go on that journey, I'm not ready or interested in a juice cleanse."

Damn. I have *for sure* been on both sides of that conversation. Have you?

I have most often been the person who is so commit-ted to what I'm experiencing that I want to share every single morsel of it with my closest people. In many of those instances I've also been the one who got my feelings hurt or became angry and resentful when I *did* share and felt rebuffed. On the flip side, I have been the one who had someone I cared about try to pull me into where *they* were on *their journey* without understanding that I was on my own path and therefore it would be impossible for us to be at the same place at the same time.

Yes, I realize I just used a story about pooping my pants to illustrate the journey of healing after loss or coming through crisis. I did it mostly because I hoped it would make you laugh, but also to remind you that it is very natural for you to want your partner or your closest people to process the way you process, at the pace you do. Others who have experienced the same trauma or crisis might try to pull you along on their journey of healing, at their pace. But as Beans so wisely put it, everyone's expe-rience is their own. Everyone's experience of loss is deeply individual, as is their decision on how to heal.

This work that you are doing is meant to be for your-self, *by yourself.* You can absolutely find strength and courage to walk through hard things so that you can be stronger for the people you love—but nobody can do the work for you. And nobody can tell you how it can be done. Not even me. All you can do is gather the tools you are presented with and choose those that serve your needs best.

## THINGS THAT HELPED ME

**SET YOUR INTENTIONS FOR YOUR JOURNEY:** The older I get the more I understand that I get to choose how I do anything, including the hardest seasons. Now when I face something hard, once the initial shock has worn off, I challenge myself to set my intentions for my process. As my marriage is dissolving, I have challenged myself to stay present in the pain so that I can fully process it. I have identified how I want to show up for myself and my children—going so far as to explicitly list how I want to care for myself, where I need to hold firm to boundaries, and how I want to show up for the people I love most. By giving myself a path I feel a sense of calm even in the midst of chaos and on the hardest days I can remind myself of who I am.

*GET YOURSELF A JUDGMENT-FREE ZONE*: As much as you're on an individual journey, it's still important that you have someone to process with: judgment free. I have the most incredible squad and we regularly get together to talk about anything and everything. Within our group there is never judgment. Accountability? Yes, but judgment? Never. It's a safe place where people accept me as I am, for who I truly am, and where I don't censor myself. If you don't have a space where you can do that, you can find a group online (anonymity might be helpful) or even inside the pages of a journal. When we keep our feelings locked up they work like a pressure cooker. The more you try to suppress them the more the pressure grows until it bursts, causing way more damage than if you'd just had the courage to admit the truth in the first place.

*GO FIRST*: Maybe you read the idea above and you're, like, *Well, that's great for you, Rach, but I don't have a crew like that!* Actually, you might totally have great people like that in your life, but you've just never had a conversation with them that's deeper than a puddle.

My friend Brad is one of the oldest souls I know and the most accepting of every kind of person he comes into contact with . . . but there's a caveat—he can't stand small talk. If he's chatting with another person, even the clerk at the grocery store, he wants to connect with them. Brad could be in the cereal aisle (except he would never eat processed food or gluten) and if someone started talking to him about their struggles with their mom, I swear he would stand there until nightfall discussing every single detail that person wanted to share. I'm not suggesting that you start wandering the aisles of Trader Joe's looking for a confidant, but I am suggesting that you start opening up to the people in your life to see if there's any *there* there. You don't have to unload every thought and feeling—after all, not everyone is at the place in their journey to handle authenticity. But you could begin by testing the water to see if some of the people in your life are just as willing to be as real as you are.

# 3

## LET GO OF GUILT

I wrote this entire book from the perspective of when bad things or hard times or crisis happens *to us*—since that is the experience I am having. But I've realized in the edit, and in the season that I find myself currently, that there is an entirely different perspective I haven't taken into account.

What if your world shatters, not because of something out of your control, but because **you** broke it? What if you aren't just drowning in pain—what if you're the one who caused the pain in the first place? What if guilt is the biggest form of suffering you now endure, and something you can't escape because the shame of your actions is eating you alive?

Maybe you feel guilty because you've deeply wronged someone. Maybe you cheated. Maybe you treated someone unfairly. Maybe you bullied. Maybe you lied. Maybe you used. Maybe you abandoned. Maybe you destroyed their faith and their trust in you again and again. I can't know exactly what it is that you did or how specifically you hurt them but here's what I do know—if you feel guilt and shame about it now, and you're facing the reality that you did something wrong even though that feeling is extremely uncomfortable, it means you're *trying*. You may never receive forgiveness from the person or people you hurt, but you can do the work to forgive yourself.

Your holding on to your shame will not undo what was done. There is no amount of self-flagellation that will rewind the present back to the past. All we can ever do is our best to make it right, and then our best to understand why we caused the pain so that we might never do so again. If you're reading this and you're trapped in self-hatred from something that you've done, I beg you to remember that hatred never heals—only love can do that. You are going to have to love yourself enough to seek help. You are going to have to love yourself enough to forgive yourself. You are going to have to love yourself enough to believe that you can be better, that you *will be* better, next time.

You are also going to have to love yourself enough to walk away from anyone who weaponizes your guilt and uses it against you.

Years ago, I was working with a married couple during one of our conferences—and during that conversation I held my tongue and didn't say what I was really thinking. It was earlier on in my career and I didn't yet trust my gut or my intuition to speak truthfully—especially with an audience watching this couple process the very painful parts of their relationship so publicly. But I cannot tell you how many times I have thought about that couple over the years and regretted not saying to them what I will say to you now.

Be careful that *your* guilt doesn't become *their* revenge.

This couple had been married for a few years before they began to have struggles in their marriage—they both agreed it had become strained. As often happens in moments like this at conferences, what begins as me asking a seemingly innocuous question lances a pain people have subconsciously wanted to unpack. I remember that she looked at him first, silently asking for permission to tell their story, and he nodded in agreement. Then she told us through choking sobs that she had cheated on him. He told us through choking sobs how devastated he was. That room, full of hundreds of people, fell silent as their story came furiously bubbling to the surface. I hadn't expected their response and was in no way prepared to navigate it. I continued to ask them questions to try to help them see their partner's perspective, and all the while I was praying profusely in my head. Somewhere through all of their tears she said the sentence I still can't forget. "He says he forgives me. He says he wants to start fresh and we do and it's good for a while, but then something will happen, and it always comes back to my mistake." She listed off all of the things they'd done to repair their marriage: therapy as individuals and together, counseling with their minister, and endless books and work like the conference we were in then. No matter what she did or how hard she worked he couldn't truly forgive. He was nodding along when he spoke, "I try, I try. I do love her, and I do want to forgive her but I'm so hurt—I'm just so hurt." And he was. Everyone in the room could feel his pain. I kept thinking, *They've done so much work, they've tried so many things, I don't know what else they can do* . . . Then something clicked in my mind . . . all that work had to have taken a lot of time. All that therapy and all those conferences and all those books . . . these weren't people trying for a Band-

Aid. These were people who had put in massive amounts of effort and untold hours. This realization prompted me to ask just how long they had been at this.

Years.

It had been *years,* you guys. I'm not implying that infidelity is something easily worked through, but this couple were having the same painful arguments they'd been having since the initial hurt. No matter what she did to prove to him that she was sorry and would never make the mistake again, he still reserved the right to be just as hurt by it, all those years later, as he had been originally. And what I knew then, with bone-deep clarity, was that on some level—even subconsciously—he would stay inside of this deep pain because his hurt was how he punished her for wounding him. You see, if he was angry, she might get angry too. But if he was hurt, if he was wounded and she was the cause . . . he got to hold it over her head for the rest of their lives.

I didn't say this to that couple because this man was too deep inside of his pain to even be aware of what he was doing. I didn't say it that day because on some level it felt inappropriate to tell someone wounded that he was being unfair. I didn't say it that day because she had told the room that she cheated, and it felt easier to honor her honesty than defend her right to move on from it. I didn't say what I knew, that it would be impossible for them to ever have a healthy relationship if that dynamic wasn't resolved. I didn't say it to them, though I have prayed many times over the years that someone else did.

I'm using this story to help you if you find yourself in a similar situation now. If you have sincerely apologized, if you have sincerely worked to change and continue to do so but the person you hurt continues to hold your action over your head years later—that's not forgiveness, that's manipulation. Just because you did something you deeply regret doesn't mean that you should suffer for the rest of your life. Yes, you should care that you hurt someone. Yes, you should apologize and make amends. But you shouldn't be required to carry that pain for the rest of your life and anyone who says that they forgive you wouldn't want that for you either.

**ANOTHER WAY THAT GUILT MIGHT SHOW UP FOR YOU INSIDE** of or after crisis is the guilt that *other people* think you are required to carry. It's the man who wants to date again after the loss of his wife but doesn't because his children are angry at him for moving on. It's the girl in college who finally finds the courage to admit who she really is only to be faced with the recriminations offered her by "concerned" family members.

It's the author who's written for years about working on her marriage and the Internet bullies who say horrible things when that marriage ends . . .

I don't read the comments, but somehow they find their way to me through anxious friends and family who seem to think that strangers on the Internet might get some say in my life. Sometimes the sharing is cryptic, like when my aunt will text me, "Oh Rachel, I can't believe the things they're saying about you on Facebook!" Sometimes it's specific, like people reaching out and asking for a refund to a women's conference they attended years before, due to the fact that I'm a "misleading liar" and because she thought she "was being taught by a God-fearing woman," and "Since only a sinner contemplates divorce, I rebuke everything you've taught me."

As if the pain of the decision to end our marriage isn't already hard enough, as if breaking this news to our children wasn't one of the most gut-wrenching moments of our lives, as if fighting to still be a family and still remain friends even in the midst of it all isn't nearly impossible to carry. As if the years I've spent teaching negates the fact that I am, and have only ever been, a human being navigating my way through to the best of my ability. Here is what I say to that . . . and my response isn't truly for the people who think I should carry some guilt for getting divorced; no, my response is for anyone who finds themselves trying to shake loose the shame others ask them to carry and they need a go-to response. Try this one: *I will not hold space for your expectations, your recriminations, or your judgment.*

I have fought with every ounce of my energy, every piece of my intelligence, and every bit of my faith to make my marriage great. For years. We tried individual therapy and conferences together and books and prayer. We tried sex and church and podcasts and hours and hours of communication. I tried fixing it. I tried carrying it. I tried covering up how fucking hard and utterly exhausting it was to do all the carrying. I tried allowing our friendship and our laughter and our joy in our children to cover up the parts of us that were deeply unhealthy.

And then one day, I just couldn't anymore.

I made the choice I never thought I'd make. I made the choice to hurt my children. I made the choice to disappoint our family and our community and I don't feel *one ounce* of guilt about it. I feel deep, searing pain and loss and hurt and anger, but no guilt. Guilt implies that I've done something wrong, but I know I've made the only decision possible for us to come out the other side of this whole and healthier. I made the choice. I did something that hurt my children because I would rather they experience pain now than grow up believing that our unhealthy relationship was something to emulate. I disappointed our family and our community because I don't believe that other people, no matter how much they care about me, will every truly know what goes on in my life and therefore, they don't get any say in how I live it.

I am willing to be the villain in someone else's story if it means I can be the hero of my own. I can't tell you where that proclamation leads me, I'm still deeply in the heart of this, but I do have a clarity I didn't know was possible. I cannot hurt myself to spare other people discomfort and I refuse to feel guilty for being unwilling to do so. Not anymore.

## THINGS THAT HELPED ME

**PRETEND YOU'RE COUNSELING SOMEONE ELSE:** If you're struggling under the weight of guilt and having a hard time letting it go, then let's play pretend.

Let's pretend that the thing you feel so guilty about was actually done by someone else. I want you to imagine that a friend of yours has come to you to share that they did exactly what you did. They're sick with shame and struggling to move past it. What would you tell them? What would you say to someone who finds themselves where you find yourself? Chances are you'd be way more gracious and likely, much more constructive when giving them advice than you are with yourself.

**REMEMBER THAT YOU CAN HAVE BAD THOUGHTS AND STILL BE A GOOD PERSON:** I would just like to take this moment to remind you that your having petty, small-minded, rude, impractical, greedy, selfish thoughts doesn't make you a bad person. I've thought about *Star Trek* before, that doesn't make me a Klingon. I grew up in a faith that talked about what we should think on and I've always loved the scripture *whatever is true, honorable, just, pure, lovely, etc., etc. . . . think on these things.* I love this reminder to us all to focus on the kinds of thoughts we want to have but I don't think that means we must be ashamed of the very real, human thoughts that are in there too. Emphasis on *human,* guys.

**REMEMBER THAT YOU CAN DO SOMETHING BAD AND STILL BE A GOOD PERSON:** When I was growing up, I knew my extended family had this rule about gossip—or more specifically, how old you had to be in order to be allowed to gossip. You see, my aunts and grandma looooved to sit around in Grandma's kitchen and gossip, but the rule was you weren't allowed in Grandma's kitchen to gossip until you got your period. The ladies in my family considered that to be the ultimate test of maturity and it was a huge deal for me when I was finally allowed in. I remember on one of my first visits after that rite of passage sitting around and listening to all the women talk. Specifically, one aunt was telling the rest about a friend whose husband had left her for another woman. Another aunt piped up matter-of-factly, "That's what she gets for falling in love with a scoundrel, a leopard doesn't change its spots." That was the first time I ever heard the expression about a leopard but it certainly wouldn't be the last, and many people, like my aunts, believe that expression to be true. I mean, it is a true statement when it comes to a leopard and the genetic makeup that means it was made in a certain way. But it is entirely false to state that a human being, having made a bad decision, is now locked into that decision, unchanging, for the rest of time. You are not a leopard. You are an ever-evolving being who will continue to change over time. You are whoever you decide that you are and only you are ultimately responsible for what that looks like.

WHAT TO DO

# TOMORROW

# 4

## TRY ON ANOTHER PERSPECTIVE

When I was a little girl, I believed that in order to make a baby a man put his penis in between a woman's legs and peed.

Okay, just for clarity here, I don't mean that I thought said penis went up *into* the woman, I mean that what my little kid brain knew was that he put his penis in between her thighs and peed into—well to be honest, it never occurred to me that peeing in between legs would just create a mess and not actually get anything near anywhere that might cause anything to happen—but believe it I did. Why did I believe this? Because once as a wee lass I asked my favorite aunt what sex was and she got extremely flustered and said sternly, "It's when a man puts his penis in between a woman's legs and stuff comes out of him!" and then she whirled around in a huff and got as far away from me as possible. I wasn't able to ask any follow-up questions. My eight-year-old brain immediately conjured a mental picture of what she had described and for years and years, that belief was a capital T truth in my life. Not like, a joke of what sex was, but an "I know with 100 percent clarity that this is accurate."

Also, I *knew for a fact* that if you swallowed a watermelon seed you would grow a watermelon in your belly. I *knew* that if you swallowed an apple seed you would die almost instantly. Once upon a time I *knew*, with scientific support, that Pluto was a planet. Turns out it was just a lousy dwarf planet disguising itself on the fringes of our solar system. Loser.

Think about it . . . how many things did you used to believe *with total conviction* that you now know are false? Fake? Untrue? Chances are that you've also, at one time or another, believed some things that now seem ridiculous. Only, at the time they weren't ridiculous, they were your reality—a reality that was made up, not of facts, but of the lens you viewed the world through. That lens, my friends, is your perspective.

Your Perspective—or, the way you see your life and the world around you, is an important conversation we must have right now as you come through your hard season and there are two key things you need to know about it.

The first is that your perspective on ***any and every given subject*** isn't necessarily based on the truth, but instead is based almost entirely on your past experiences and what they've taught you to think about the subject up for review. The second thing that you need to know about perspective is that *who you are in your present* is strong enough to control the beliefs you have because of your past.

You are in control of your perspective.

You are in control of your perspective! Very few people understand that. Understanding this fundamental truth won't just change the way you look at grief or pain or loss, but learning to adjust and control your perspective is the key to a happier, more centered life regardless of the season you're in.

**BUT TO UNDERSTAND THAT WE FIRST HAVE TO START WITH THE DEFINITION OF THE WORD.**

per·spec·tive

/pər'spektiv/

*noun*

*t of drawing solid objects on a two-
...sional surface so as to give the right
impression of their height, width, depth, and
position in relation to each other when viewed
from a particular point.*

*A particular attitude toward or way of
regarding something; a point of view.*

Now, when most people are talking about the idea
of perspective in regards to personal development they
will focus solely on the second definition of this word.
A *particular attitude toward something* is how you look at
the situation—literally any situation you find yourself in.

Are you afraid of dogs or do you love dogs? Why do
you feel that way?

Is money something positive or a topic that brings up
negative emotions? Why do you feel that way?

In a new relationship, are you more inclined to trust
completely at the outset or hold someone at arm's length
until they earn your trust (and sometimes even that's not
enough)? Why do you feel that way?

In every single instance—in every single situation
listed above—the way we feel about these questions, the

way we see these situations is based on a collection of past experiences. We don't tend to make conscious decisions about what to feel. Our subconscious looks at the object in front of us—a golden retriever, a mortgage, or a first date—and quickly computes whether the situation is good or bad. Based on what our subconscious tells us, our nervous system hops on the bandwagon, engaging the feeling that goes along with what your brain just told it was true.

That golden retriever? He's harmless. In fact, his name is Sebastian and he's the goodest good boy ever. Unfortunately, when you were five a neighbor's dog snapped at you and bit you. His bite lacerated your cheek, which meant a trip to the emergency room for shots and stitches—both of which terrified you. Now, thirty-two years later, you don't even consciously remember the hospital visit but you'll still cross to the other side of the street when you see a dog. In situations where you're unable to move away from a dog, or worse, one surprises you altogether, you feel intense and instantaneous fear. Your heart races and your stomach churns. Nothing, *literally nothing* is happening that should make you feel unsafe, but your perspective when it comes to dogs was written in long ago and your body is conditioned to this response. Your perspective and your body will react this way every time if you don't do anything to change the instinct.

Your perspective on dogs is just one of the thousands and thousands of beliefs you have, based on your past. Right now, whatever is happening in your life is either something negative or positive based on your perspective and the meaning you have given to it. I know that might sound hard to wrap your head around in a book on grief. But let's think this through. There's immense power in understanding that you are subconsciously coloring your reality through the lens of past experiences. If you can understand that you hold the power to perceive something as entirely negative, you harness the power to see positives in every situation too. If you are conditioned to see loss and pain as a reason to quit at life, to become bitter or withdraw, then your perspective needs to be repositioned. Try pushing the pain in the direction of rebirth, renewal, a path toward something new, even if that's scary. See what that shift gives you? Hope.

Recently I was interviewing Greg McKeown for my podcast and it was as fascinating a conversation as I could have hoped for. If you've never read Greg's book *Essentialism* please add it to your list because it's a topic everyone needs to consider. As it happened, I was interviewing him while we were both in quarantine and we were talking about the state of the world and the fear that so many were experiencing and before I could help myself I had slid out my proverbial soapbox and started a sort of rant about reaching for joy in a hard season. I can't seem to help myself in such situations because as you likely know, I feel such a deep and desperate belief that it is possible to find goodness even in hard things (see: the entire book that you're currently reading). At some point during my motivational outburst I felt a little sheepish—after all I barely knew this man, and there I was, going off at him about the silver lining.

"I sound a bit like Pollyanna," I added in. "I know I do, but I can't help myself."

"Have you ever read the story of Pollyanna?" Greg's crisp British accent made the question feel important— like a wizened professor was about to impart something powerful. And I suppose that's exactly what happened.

"No, I honestly can't say that I have," I told him. I only know Pollyanna as a reference I've heard again and again—usually aimed at me, and often as something negative. As in, *Rachel, stop acting like such a Pollyanna!*

Greg went on to explain that he hadn't actually either but that his wife had read it to their children, and he'd listened.

"Pollyanna turns a negative into a positive at least a hundred times in that book," he told me. "That's not something to be ashamed of, that's something to be admired. A person who can turn a negative into a positive can never be defeated. It's a super-power."

Your ability to control your perspective, your ability to take a negative and flip it on its head and find meaning inside of it—that's a super-power!

But how do you do that if you haven't spent years building up that skill? That's where the second definition of the word comes into play. The art of drawing solid objects on a two-dimensional surface so that your eyes don't play tricks on you.

When we were still fresh-faced newlyweds Dave and I saved up our money and went to Europe for the first time. The whole trip was a bit of a disaster; in an age before smartphones, traveling to multiple countries in Europe without much money was sketchy at the best of times. But we were young and in love and we have always had (and still continue to have) the most fun together even if we're lost and broke (we were both throughout that trip). In order to save money on airfare we decided to drive from Rome to Venice—in Italy, you guys. It just so happened that we ended up in Pisa on Thanksgiving Day. I remember it was Thanksgiving because we ate lunch at a McDonald's—a location our painful lack of culture (and painfully American perspective on quality food!) made it feel like it was the right choice in one of the greatest food destinations on the planet—and after a Quarter Pounder with cheese we hightailed it over to the leaning tower. What's shocking about the leaning tower of Pisa is that it's actually much smaller than you'd imagine. My recollection is that, while yes, it is in fact leaning, it's also just a little bell tower in the courtyard of a local cathedral. For some reason I'd imagined it as more of a skyscraper or at least the height of a moderately sized Ramada Inn. If you have held a similar notion, let me tell you something upsetting—Texas has gas station billboards taller than that tower. While its height leaves something to be desired, we were there, right? So, we had to get "the picture." You know the one. It's like you're required by tourist law to get the silly photo with that tower that messes with the viewer's perspective. People adjust themselves so that when the final shot is revealed, it appears as if they're hugging the tower or leaning against it or a dozen other angles that make it seem as if they're the same size as the building. By adjusting where they're standing on *the two-dimensional surface* our perspective is fooled into believing that something is bigger than it actually is. Hilarity ensues. I'm sad to say that shot near the beginning of our trip was the impetus for a myriad of altered perspective photos; no European landmark was spared. The Eiffel tower became something small enough that it fit between both my hands. The Colosseum became something to lean against since it was exactly my height. An ancient cannon on display in London? That became an unmentionable massively oversized appendage that we're immature enough to still cackle about when we see the picture today.

An object *appearing* bigger than it really actually is changed the way we were able to view reality.

So . . . which parts of your life are you seeing as much bigger than they have any right to be? What are the areas that are causing suffering that, if you were able to adjust the way you were looking at them, would cease to matter as much? How can you rethink your negative experiences as happening FOR you and not TO you? And how can you stop letting the negative experiences of your past keep you from healing from the trauma you are currently facing? Because isn't each experience its very own, unique, moment in your life?

## THINGS THAT HELPED ME

**ASK YOURSELF IF THIS IS REAL:** When past experiences are affecting the way we look at a situation, it's incredibly difficult to even realize it's happening. It's so easy to get swept into the feeling without ever identifying what's triggering it in the first place. A simple question that I ask myself when this occurs is, did the thing that I'm upset about *really happen*? Our minds are incredibly powerful and if you're not careful just thinking about the possibility of something bad happening can make us feel as if something bad has happened. Asking the question might not immediately make the feeling I'm having go away, but it does ground me back into the present so I can start to get clarity.

**STEP OUTSIDE OF YOUR PERSPECTIVE:** Once I've asked myself whether it's really happening, I can separate myself from the thoughts I'm having.

Anyone who has ever suffered from anxiety or panic knows how easy it is to be controlled by the thoughts you're having, so a separation is key to change the way you're thinking and feeling. Even a momentary pause in the way you have been considering things can give you the space you need to make a shift.

*SEE IF YOU CAN MAKE THE OPPOSITE TRUE*: Once I'm able to think it through I challenge myself to come at it from a different angle than the one that was making me feel something negative . . . ideally, I try and see if I can't find a way for *the opposite of what I'm thinking* to also be true. For instance, the first few weeks we were in quarantine I felt all kinds of negative emotions: fear, anxiety, bitterness, and anger would all bubble up throughout the days. That's no way to live. Even though I do feel negative emotions I will never allow myself to wallow in them. I forced myself to step outside the way I was thinking and feeling and see if there was another way to look at it. Instead of thinking of the quarantine as something bad that I had to endure I challenged myself to ask how the opposite could be true and it hit me right between the eyes. Quarantine is a privilege. There were millions of people who weren't able to quarantine or socially distance because of socioeconomic reasons. During the time that I was complaining, there were parents who were caring for critically ill children and they were wishing that their biggest concern in life was whether or not there would be milk at the grocery store that week. There were essential workers, exhausted beyond belief, who toiled around the clock to keep our society running, and those people would have given anything to be stuck inside their homes on a rainy day trying to occupy their kids. It was like flipping a light switch from off to on. Once I had this newfound perspective, I couldn't ever go back to the way I'd been seeing things before. Once you can prove to yourself that the opposite of your viewpoint is true, it challenges the beliefs you were clinging to and forces you to see the world differently.

**ARM YOURSELF WITH EXAMPLES OF THE PERSPECTIVE
YOU WANT:** It's crucial that you surround yourself
with the influence of people who think and act
the way you want to think and act. If you're
going through something difficult and everyone
around you only affirms how justified you are in
the misery you won't ever have the opportunity to
consider another angle. Look for teachers, writers,
artists, and speakers who have the perspective
you'd like to have or even have just processed
a similar situation to yours in a way that you
haven't. Research and collect as many different
ideas and tools as you can. Fill your awareness
with positivity and light, not because life is
perfect or easy but because your mind is fully
qualified to tell you all the reasons why today was
awful—you need the influence of others, perhaps
those who aren't in such a hard place, to remind
you that although life does sometimes suck, it's
also pretty damn awesome too.

# 5

## CHANGE YOUR MIND ABOUT GETTING BETTER

Now that we've gotten around the notion of perspective and how it colors how we look at things, let's go a bit further. Let's get into the idea of mindset. Perspective and mindset are incredibly similar because both are influenced by our past and both are pieces of ourselves we are fully in control of. *But* there is a distinct difference between the two. Perspective is the way you *see* the world. Mindset is what you *think* about what you see.

I like to think of mindset as an unformed piece of clay. Personally, I don't have a ton of experience with pottery save the one time in fifth-grade art class when we were allowed to create something for Mother's Day. Each of us was given a blob of gray clay and tasked with turning it into anything—literally anything—our ten-year-old selves thought our mothers would love.

I made a puffin.

While other kids created rough-hewn bowls to hold jewelry or coffee cups that were decidedly *not* seaworthy, I made an Atlantic puffin.

I know what you must be thinking . . . *How precious, her mother collected puffin figurines and baby Rachel decided to add to the menagerie.* Not exactly. My mother has never one time taken an interest in puffins—Atlantic or otherwise—but fifth-grade me had recently learned about them and I wanted to try my hand at a faithful re-creation. I was utterly captivated by their adorable squatty body and multicolored beak. The piece turned out just darling, I'll admit, and my mother seemed to like it, but sadly that is my single experience with personal pottery making. The only other knowledge I have on the subject, I learned through Patrick Swayze.

If you've never had the fortune of experiencing the movie *Ghost,* I'm sad for you because it is a masterpiece. In that movie Patrick Swayze is married to Demi Moore and through a series of unfortunate events he becomes a ghost and then teams up with Whoopi Goldberg to solve the mystery of his own death. That stuff is good. But the great moment? If you've seen it, you and I *both* know it's that scene at the potter's wheel. If memory serves me correctly, Demi is an artist and she's sitting with the wheel making something out of clay when Patrick comes up behind her and the Righteous Brothers start playing and clay goes from PG to R-rated *real* fast. It's epic and I don't care what anybody says, nothing gets close to the panache of an R-rated make-out scene from the nineties!

Sigh.

That's not the point, though; the focus of this story is on the unformed clay that Demi and Patrick are inappropriately manipulating on that wheel. That's what I want you to imagine when it comes to your mindset. Not the inappropriate stuff, you dirty bird. The clay.

The absolute greatest book on this subject is by Carol Dweck and it's called *Mindset* and please, please, *please* add it to your TBR pile if you want to take a deeper dive. The gist of the book is the idea that we all have one of two mindsets. A fixed mindset: meaning that you believe that whatever talents, skills, knowledge, or abilities you have are fixed and cannot be changed. Or you have a growth mindset: meaning that you believe that you can develop new talents, learn new skills, gain more knowledge and abilities for as long as you're on the planet. Fixed mindset people have a past that shapes their perspective—the way they see the world around them (there's that *perspective* word again)—and, here's the kicker, **they don't believe it's possible to make themselves different or better**. When they see people grow or change or achieve in ways they can't, they believe that those people are "just wired differently."

Dave spent most of his life with a fixed mindset and as he wrote in his book, he has actively worked for years to change this. On the flip side, I have always had a growth mindset. Not on purpose. Honestly, I didn't even know the words for what to call this part of my personality until I read Carol Dweck's book, I just truly have always believed I could do anything if I tried hard enough. By contrast my husband grew up believing he could do as much as he was capable of doing but that it was limited by what was already inside of him. The interesting thing is that Dave and I had wildly different childhoods. For all intents and purposes, everything about the way I grew up reinforced how little access I had to resources, how few people supported me, how very harsh life could be. And yet, I think there was something about everything I *didn't have* that made me view the world as a puzzle to figure out. At a very early age I came to the conclusion that the only thing standing in between me and anything I desired was knowledge I didn't yet possess. I also believed that if I was willing to work hard and continue to study, that I could learn how to do anything better. I've approached every area of my life this way: business, certainly, my mental and emotional health, how to be a better parent, how to be kinder to myself. People laugh at our conferences when I tell them that the secret of my success is Google, but it is the absolute truth. Every single thing I know I fought to learn. Dave on the other hand was naturally smart, talented, and charming and he had two loving parents who encouraged him to live into his abilities. He grew up in a middle-class neighborhood in the suburbs of Southern California and while he worked hard in his life, as a straight, white, Christian man living in America, there wasn't a lot of opposition and therefore not much of anything to overcome. What many people would see as advantages in his childhood would end up hindering him as an adult—when you believe your talents and skills are natural and God-given, you'll never learn to push past the perceived limits you see as preordained.

Imagine that clay again—think of your mindset as

a formless piece of clay and this time, instead of Demi, *you're* the potter mushing it with your hands. (If you need to imagine Patrick sitting behind you, shirtless, go ahead. I won't ask questions.) As you form it, that piece of clay can become a vase or a coffee mug or a bowl or a puffin. You can work with it and turn it into any shape you imagine and then re-form it into something new and different. So long as you continue to work with it and continue to add more clay or more water it can grow and change and exist forever in the state of *becoming*.

That's a growth mindset.

As long as you keep adding new ideas, experiences, challenges, talents, and skills you will forever be able to alter the way you think about what you see.

If we're using unformed clay as an analogy for a growth mindset you might think that a fixed mindset is clay after its been fired in the kiln. After all, when a potter is done with their work, they set the piece permanently by baking it in a fire. Once they understand that they have a fixed mindset, most people who own up to it will fight back against this notion. *I never chose to stop growing*, they'll say, *I didn't permanently set anything.* But here's the thing: you can bake the clay and make a purposeful choice to lock it into that form forever but that's not the only way to set it in stone. The other way to commit to a fixed state is by not touching the thing at all. Think about it, even with my limited knowledge of pottery, even I know that if you don't keep working the clay, if you just leave it sitting out in the open unattended and uncared for, it will dry out and turn brittle and hard all on its own. I don't believe people with a fixed mindset consciously choose to live this way. I believe the way they've been programmed to think makes them believe that there isn't any other option. Their perspective has them trapped.

So why do I bring this up here, in the context of living through pain? Because when I ponder the notion of trying to work through hard things while holding on to a fixed mindset, I can't even imagine how awful that must feel. A difficult season is already painful enough without the added weight of a belief system that tells you it's hopeless before you even try to find your way out.

You *can* get through this. There *is* hope. You will not always feel the way you feel today.

The worst of the worst stuff that can happen to us as humans? Not a unique experience. No matter what it is that you're going through, I promise you that somebody has walked that road ahead of you and turned back to give others clues about how to navigate the path. Will every one of those guides be right for you? Of course not. But some of them will. Some of them will have ideas or tips or advice that will help you take one step and then another and another after that. If you believe there are lessons in the world that will help you heal, and you're willing to go looking, you will find them. If you don't believe these lessons exist, you will never look. You won't discover them. And your healing . . . well, that process is going to be much more difficult for you.

You can make a decision to stay here and stay stuck, you can let your clay sit and dry out. But make no mistake, choosing to do nothing is a choice in and of itself. There's an old scripture (and an old Byrds song) that tells us there is a season for everything. A season to laugh, a season to cry, and yes, a season for grief. Allow yourself that season of grief. Allow yourself to feel and process as you need to. But when you're ready to move past that season, when you want to look for hope and look for help and look for guidance . . . that's out there too. Unless you have a growth mindset, you'll watch that season pass you by.

A fixed mindset will tell you that you've been dealt a crappy hand and this is just your lot in life. A growth mindset (which is something you *can* develop even if it feels uncomfortable and not natural for you) will tell you (if you listen) that there are answers, there is help, if you're willing to go seek it out.

## THINGS THAT HELPED ME

**RESEARCH SPECIFIC PROBLEMS:** I think the reason people struggle so much with finding solutions to their struggles is that they cast a wide net for a narrow problem. For instance, if you're going through a divorce and you read books on divorce, you're taking on which parts of divorce the author thought were most important. They are specific to that author, not to you or your real life. Instead of casting a wide net like "best books for divorce," focus instead on the areas you're struggling with the most. Abandonment or betrayal or learning to co-parent or trust or fidelity. There are a hundred different approaches to learn about the thing you're going through, that feel tough to you specifically, so dig into the topic you need, not just the category.

**LEARN IN THE WAY THAT WORKS BEST FOR YOU:** I
spoke about this a ton in *Girl, Stop Apologizing* but
the gist is, personal development is supposed to
be *personal*. If you try and absorb information in
a way that works for others but feels hard for you
it's a waste of time. For instance, I love to read. I
read more books than you can imagine and I geek
out on little tiny details of nonfiction books to add
tools to my tool kit. If you get bored or lost reading
a book then it doesn't matter how good the book is
or how much it might help you, you're not going to
take it in. Instead ask yourself how *you* learn best.
Maybe you want to research podcasts on the topic.
Maybe you want to watch YouTube videos. Maybe
there's digital classes online you can dive into or a
workbook to write in or some art therapy you can
look into. It doesn't matter *how* you take in the
information just so long as you do.

**TRY A DIFFERENT APPROACH:** One of the telltale signs
of a fixed mindset is the belief that when you try
one thing and it doesn't work it means there isn't
an answer. For instance, when my brother died my

parents thought it would be a good idea for me and my sisters to go to group therapy with other people who had lost someone. I hated that idea. Please don't get me wrong, group therapy can be amazing, but I'm not someone who feels comfortable processing big emotions like that in a room full of strangers. Also, I wasn't sure how to hear about other people's loss and not have it make my own feel even greater. Group therapy wasn't the answer for me, but one-on-one therapy has saved my mental health more times than I can count. If you try to make a change or learn something new or get past a hard topic and it doesn't work, don't assume there isn't an answer or that something is wrong with you, just try something else. If that doesn't work, try something different again. Keep trying different approaches until you find an idea that helps.

# 6

## HACK YOUR COURAGE

I'm afraid of a surprising number of things.

Let me clarify. I'm not afraid of big things: I've moved away from home and started a whole new life. Twice. I quit my job and started my own company . . . seventeen years and going strong. I wrote books even when nobody read them. I've given birth three times and fought through years of the adoption process to hold my daughter in my arms. When it's big things, I seem to have no end of courage. But little stuff? I'm actually kind of a weenie.

Skiing, snowboarding, water skis—basically anything involving me going faster than humans were meant to go, while riding on top of some kind of *blade*? Absolutely not.

I hate public restrooms because I live in fear of someone walking in on me using the toilet. The only thing worse than someone walking in while I'm on the potty is someone doing it on the *one day* I thought it would be cute to wear a jumpsuit. Because now they've not only seen my hoo haw, they're also trying to figure out why I take off all my clothes just to pee.

Snakes are abhorrent.

Big Foot (okay, the *idea* of Big Foot) is too much for me to handle.

Aliens? I just threw up in my mouth.

I *refuse* to even glance at a mirror in the dark because I heard about Bloody Mary when I was at a slumber party as a child and am now scarred for life.

How about El Chupacabra? El Cuco? La Llorona?! I grew up in a community with a large Hispanic population, which means I've got the childhood fears of two cultures!

Airplane toilet seat somehow suctioning to my body and then sucking my intestines out into the air? Something that's given me pause more than once.

I'm afraid of *many* things. Not all of them real, even. I want you to remember all of the things I just listed because we're going to talk about courage—and the thing you need to really understand about it is that having courage isn't the same as being fearless. There are so many great things that great people in history have said about courage and fear, but the one that resonates most with me is from Franklin Delano Roosevelt. He said, "Courage is not the absence of fear, but rather the assessment that something else is more important than fear." Take that in. Think about that.

In the case of all those tiny little things I tend to be so afraid of, I never seek out anything to override the fear because they're inconsequential. I don't go through life worried that the aliens in *Signs* are going to take me out—not anymore, anyway—so I don't need to do a ton of work to overcome that particular concern. Big Foot is just folklore. Deep down I know this, so I still go into the woods from time to time. Most snakes aren't poisonous even if they are disgusting. See what I mean?

But there are plenty of times when our fear can be crippling and it's usually a result of the reminder of the pain we've experienced before. We fear loving again because of the potential to be hurt again. We fear putting ourselves out there because last time we were rejected. Now the pain isn't only a harsh instance in our past, it's controlling our actions in the present and our possibility in the future. When we go through something difficult or encounter a big life change it takes courage to move forward in any way. Meaning, in order to move forward you must decide that there is something greater at stake than the way you're feeling or your fear of feeling pain again.

Did you get that?

You must decide that there is something greater at stake than your fear!

Please note that I didn't say, *You will realize in time that something* . . . No. I said you must **decide**. You must make a choice to go forward in faith, not in fear. And not only that, but you're going to have to choose again and again, especially on the hard days.

To me, choosing courage in an awful season is sort of like having a five-week-old baby. Yes, guys, I know I use mom analogies a lot in my writing, but you write what you know, and also this is a good one, I swear. I assume that many of you have experienced the joy (and the pain) of having a five-week-old baby, but let me paint a picture for those of you who have not, and as a reminder for those of you whose kids are so long out of the house that maybe the fog of time has dulled the edges of this hell.

Five weeks old is past the point of the initial eupho-ria. Now, don't get me wrong. You're still crazy obsessed with your baby and so happy to have them out in the world wearing the teeny, tiny clothes you spent months collecting and then washing in that special newborn de-tergent. But at five weeks, the initial adrenaline rush has worn off enough that you start to feel the hard stuff too. You feel the exhaustion from no sleep. If you have more than one child, you feel the stress of trying to manage multiple needs on your limited energy supply. At five weeks in, most friends have stopped bringing you casse-roles and if your mom came into town, at five weeks she's back home again. At five weeks, you're in it and it's good but also really, really hard. But here's the thing about that time . . . no matter how tired you are, no matter how tough it seems, when that baby wakes up for the tenth time tonight you still find the will to take care of him.

When we were going through our adoption journey, we got placement of twin girls who were both born ad-dicted. My husband and I walked the halls of our house all night long with those babies. Because they were work-ing drugs from their system they wanted to be held con-stantly and it seemed like the second you got one of them settled the other would wake up screaming. It was the most exhausted I've ever been in my life—the kind of tired you feel in your bones. At many points during that time, just as I had with my sons and later my daughter, it seemed like I might collapse from lack of sleep. But you know what? Every single time those babies cried . . . every single time Jackson cried or Sawyer cried or Ford and Noah cried, I got out of bed and took care of them. I loved on them and fed them and changed hundreds of diapers. I swaddled them and rocked them even when it felt impossible. I found a way. I found something that was *greater than* my exhaustion and that was my children.

If you're struggling to find courage it isn't because you aren't brave—it's simply that you haven't identified something as more important than your fear. In a hard season, fear looms large because fear is a cousin to grief. Fear keeps you stuck in your grief too. It keeps you in the loop of remembering what happened, who you lost, who betrayed you or who you hurt. It keeps you in suspended animation at the point in which the life you had blew up and became unrecognizable to you. Fear might even be comfortable. It takes courage to get uncomfortable, especially when you've already endured a type of pain that rocked you to your core.

You may not yet have found the thing that is more important than your fear . . . but you might also, deep down, believe that there's a safety net.

Think about it. When Dave and I were taking care of our babies we were their only hope. Like Obi-Wan and the Rebel Alliance. There wasn't another option, there wasn't a Plan B, there was no one else. We found the will and the strength to carry on against crippling exhaustion because our children were incredibly important and also, there wasn't any backup. I bring this up because when people tell me they can't find the "motivation" to change, my first instinct is to tell them to attach it to something bigger than themselves. When they reply and tell me they have figured out that motivation and that they're fighting for something greater than themselves but it's still not working . . . then it's because they don't really, truly *have* to change. Maybe good is good enough. Maybe you can halfway show up as a parent because you know your kids have your partner to help them, and grandparents too. Maybe you lost the career that you loved, so you'll spend the rest of your life in another job you hate because it pays the bills. Maybe you'll live in your grief for the next five years because you gave everything to caring for your ill parent, and you lost both them and yourself in the process—and now you've decided you've got nothing left to give anyone, regardless of what that decision does to the people who are counting on you. Maybe you'll stay the enabler in your codependent relationship because the comfort of what you know—even when it's awful—is better than the fear of what would happen to you, and to them, if you found the courage to leave.

You're never going to find the courage or the strength to push past your fear if it isn't absolutely necessary. Change is hard and by definition, in order for courage to exist, you have to be working against something that scares you. I know it seems like a heavy lift to face fear in times of grief. Neither of those decisions are easy to make and so, if you don't have to and/or if something isn't more important, you will stay exactly as you are. But with courage, and only with courage, will you see all your life can be, even after your loss.

## THINGS THAT HELPED ME

**KNOW THAT YOU CAN FIGURE IT OUT:** I know I talked about this already, you guys, but if there's one reason for why I'm able to have courage so often,

it's intrinsically tied to my growth mindset.
I believe that even when I get it wrong, I learn
*something* about how to do it right and
I am less afraid. I never assume I have all of
the answers and so there isn't any pressure to do
things perfectly. Because of that I'm willing to
try anything when I know I have work to do or
something to change in my life. Sometimes my
courage is big and bold and sometimes it's small
inches forward that build on each other until they
create the distance that I need. If my first attempt
doesn't work how I hope it will, I know that I can
always try again in a different way until I figure
it out.

**STUDY THE COURAGEOUS:** It's so much easier to do
something if you can read stories about others who
have done it before you. When I'm trying to find
courage as an entrepreneur, I read books written by
other entrepreneurs. When I'm trying to learn to be
a better parent, I read books written by the kinds
of parents I admire. If you want to act in a certain
way, it's important to see that modeled for you. I've

turned to history books again and again because there are so many examples of female leaders and warriors who fought valiantly for the things they believed in and it never ceases to inspire me to be brave. So many times, women have pushed through loss, heartache, the most incredible kinds of grief you can imagine, and done world-changing things because their courage was more powerful than their fear. Read about Sojourner Truth, Harriet Tubman, Benazir Bhutto, Sacagawea. These are women who shaped the history of the world and their stories are beyond inspiring.

*FACE YOUR FEAR ALREADY!:* Look, the longer you hesitate the bigger the fear becomes and the more the anxiety can take hold. I recommend you grab your favorite notebook and write down what scares you in black and white: ***The thing I am afraid of most right now is . . .*** And then fill in the blank. Have the courage to be brutally honest with yourself. Are you afraid of losing another loved one? Of getting rejected and left behind? Of feeling vulnerable? Of people only identifying you by the tragedy you've endured? Whatever it is, just claiming it and writing it down will remove a lot of its power. Now, after you've written down that fear I want you to follow it up with this: ***And if that happens, I'll . . .*** Once you write that answer do it again: ***And once that happens, I'll . . .*** Just keep asking yourself questions and answering them. So much of your fear is of the unknown and if you can just give yourself a road map for your hypothetical scenario, you will feel more empowered. Believe me.

# 7

## *SHOW UP*

I want to take the courage conversation further. I feel like it's important now to talk about *why* you should fight for courage rather than doing nothing at all. I also feel like I should probably warn you, this topic gets me really fired up. Not "fired up" like we're the Rancho Carne Toros and we're trying to compete at nationals with a whole new routine we created after realizing that all our moves were stolen from the East Compton Clovers. No, I mean fired up as in, this topic really pushes my buttons. Actually I'll tell you the truth because that's what I do. It doesn't just push my buttons, it royally pisses me off. Good manners say that you should never come at someone who's going through something hard. But truthfully, if what I'm about to say applies to you, you need someone to be real with you and the people in your life love you too much to do it. I love you too, but I love you enough to speak the truth even if it hurts your feelings. So here goes.

Stop wallowing.

It's time. If you want to begin to move forward, then you *must* stop wallowing in despair and take the next right step to help you move forward. And before you dismiss what I'm saying as a harsh directive of a privileged author speaking about something she doesn't understand, you should know that the grown-up, mature part of me isn't the one who has such strong opinions on this issue. My *vehement* belief that you need to show the hell up for your life before it's too late comes straight from my childhood. More specifically, I'm writing this from the perspective of a little girl who didn't have the power or authority to say these things to the grown-ups in her life when she needed those grown-ups the most. I couldn't express these feelings back then, I didn't even have the language to articulate them, but many years have come and gone between then and now—enough for me to understand that what happened was wrong. So, this is me, *an adult,* telling you, *an adult,* what someone should have said to my parents long ago.

You must find the courage to keep going. *You have a responsibility to anyone who relies on you but if you're a parent, you especially owe it to your children.*

When my big brother committed suicide, it destroyed our family. Not that we were much of a family to begin with, if I'm being truthful, but whatever tenuous threads held us together were burned to ash when Ryan died. As a mother, I literally cannot imagine how awful it was for my parents to lose their only son that way. I can honor them, in that I will never, ever grasp how terrible their unique grief was. But I can also acknowledge that both my parents gave up that day. They didn't give up at life; I truly respect the fact that they both have fought hard in the years since to rebuild a life for themselves. What they did give up on after that horrific day was me. They gave up on any attempts to parent me for the remainder of my life.

I was fourteen years old.

I was fourteen years old and had just found my big brother after he put a handgun to his temple and blew his brains out against his bedroom wall. And my parents never parented me again. I have had more conversations with my eleven-year-old about Fortnite than either of my parents have ever had with me about anything I saw that day or the grief I felt or how scared I was—in the twenty-three years since.

While I had always taken care of myself (the chaos of our home necessitated it), the day my brother died was the last time either parent made any kind of real attempt at what constituted the nurturing of a child. I'm honestly not sure if either of them was emotionally stable enough in the remaining years of my childhood to even consider it. I had three Thanksgivings and three Christmases and three birthdays left at home until I moved away at seventeen years old and escaped. I know the number because each was more awful than the one before it—a stark contrast to the holidays of my childhood, which are some of the only good memories I have of my family. Holidays were the only times when everyone got along—or at least pretended to. The first Christmas after Ryan died should in theory have been the worst of them because it was so close to his death. We had some gifts—I remember acting like a pack of Kirkland tube socks were all I had been dreaming of because it was one of the few things wrapped up for me under the tree and I didn't want to hurt my mom's feelings. In retrospect I wonder if all those gifts were just easy things they could grab and wrap up during a trip to Costco. The day only got worse from there, but I realize that it isn't my place to talk about how my mother and father each handled their grief in different ways. That isn't my story to tell. *My story* is what it feels like to be left behind. *My story* is what it's like when the three daughters still living would never be enough against the loss of their only son.

The holidays closest to his loss were searing; the palpable grief in the air certainly made Ryan's absence feel all the more painful. But I can tell you now that those first holidays didn't hurt nearly as badly as the ones that came after. Even as a fourteen-year-old I could understand that our grief would mar us for a while. What I never could have anticipated was the apathy when it came to my parents' interest in parenting me that grew with each passing month.

The Christmas of my seventeenth year—this would be the fourth Christmas without my brother—was truly the darkest. I had moved to L.A. that fall and came home only for the holiday. My parents were in the process of their divorce at that point, another piece of grief for them to add to many others—especially since they'd been breaking up and getting back together for nearly a decade by then. How they spent their time or processed this new hardship is again not my story to tell, but the disinterest in being present for the holidays with us is. Since they split up there was no "home" for us to go home to that year, so I opted to crash with my sister Melody. I'm not sure if they both just assumed the other parent would celebrate with us but neither one did anything. Not one thing. I'm sure we must have seen them at a relative's house or maybe stopped by their apartments for a visit, but my only memory of Mama and Daddy during that holiday was the extreme hurt I felt at how clear it was that neither one of them cared about the holiday at all. My oldest sister was living in another state at that point, so it was just Mel and me. We didn't have money to do anything special, so we huddled up in the bed of her tiny apartment and watched *A Christmas Story* over and over on a loop on TBS. That tradition still exists to this day, twenty years later. Even grown up with families of our own, both Melody and I still play *A Christmas Story* on repeat throughout Christmas Day. When Dave and I were first married he thought I watched it on repeat each year because it was my favorite movie—the truth is, that movie serves as a reminder. That seventeenth year was the last time I went "home" for Christmas and the last time I ever will. That movie was something we used to self-soothe rather than admit that we had nowhere to go and no parents who considered it their job to create even some semblance of a celebration for us. Or even to worry about how or where we spent the holiday. During that trip home, I'm sure that we went to our grandparents' for a visit or stopped by to see our favorite aunt on her birthday but if you've ever been alone like that on Christmas Eve and Christmas Day, then you know there is a big difference between visiting someone else's house *during* the holidays and having a home at which to *spend* the holidays. No amount of visiting with people later makes up for the lack.

My oldest will be fourteen in a few months, the same age I was when my parents stopped being parents. I cannot fathom leaving a child his age alone to fend for himself. I can't fathom a world where I wouldn't *at least try.* I can't imagine disappearing into myself and leaving him to figure out the rest of his life on his own.

I want to be clear on this point. I am not suggesting for one second that you aren't allowed to grieve when you have lost something or feel anxiety or fear or frustration. We are all human—even Mama and Daddy—and as such, we'll all process hardship in our own way. But. And this is a big *but.* There is a time for grief and there is a time when you must begin showing up for your life again.

Remember earlier when I told you that sometimes what you need to be courageous is the understanding that there is no alternative? My parents had an alternative. Their alternative was knowing that I would fend for myself because I always had. The years that followed Ryan's death were the worst of my life—which is saying something, considering all the things that came after. I survived that time, certainly, and it made me so strong—of course it did. But sometimes, when the hurt bubbles up or I remember having to deal with things no teenager should be asked to, I feel rage.

I have been working on this for twenty-three years in therapy and so I understand that I feel this angry because the true emotion, deep sadness, will never feel like a safe emotion for me to attach to people who made me feel unsafe. Anger at least makes me feel empowered, but to feel sadness forces me to acknowledge an attachment to outcome I wish could have been. When it comes to my relationship with my parents, I've found that hoping for something more only ever ends in me feeling disappointed and hurt all over again.

I am telling you all of this now not to air dirty laundry but because I am positive that someone reading this is a parent who is so trapped in their own grief that they've checked out. I'm positive that someone reading this is so consumed by their own pain that they've stopped caring if the people they love are in pain as well. And so they are allowing the people they love to suffer in a way that will affect their relationship with them for the rest of their lives. I will risk pissing off my entire family with the truth if it means you wake up.

You are supposed to be the adult here!

Your kids did not ask for this pain either and now it's doubly harsh because the person who is supposed to be taking care of them is lost. Don't lie to yourself and think that because you have the support of family or friends that there's someone to cover for you. I had aunts and uncles and grandparents who loved me dearly, but as a teenager, even though I hated how my parents were acting, I was still deeply protective of them. I didn't want anyone to know how bad things at home really were. I didn't want anyone to know when I'd been alone at the house for days on end. Instead I did what I'd always done—I took care of myself and was grateful for whatever attention they gave me when they did.

There is no replacement for you as a parent. Show up! I don't care that it's hard. I don't care that it feels impossible. Your kids are counting on you—there is no plan B.

Your kids are not old enough to carry your pain for you, but I promise you they will try.

I was talking to an acquaintance recently who was going through an awful divorce and she's been a self-confessed emotional wreck for months because of it. I was asking how her daughters (a senior in high school and freshman in college) were handling everything and she told me, "They're so great, so strong. I mean . . . they've had to hear so much from me, probably heard more and seen more than they should have, but they're old enough to know the truth. They can handle it."

Nope.

I'll tell you what I told her that day. *Your kids are never old enough to watch you have a breakdown.* Your kids are never, ever old enough for you—the parent—to process your pain, grief, fear, and anxieties *with them.* Never. It is not your child's job to hold space for you to fall apart. Call your therapist, your priest, your rabbi, or your best friend but don't you dare ask your kids to carry you through a hard season. It is your job to be strong for them, even if you have to fake it. That's what you signed up for.

You do not owe everyone that—but you owe it to some people. Your people. You owe it to your team at work. You owe it to your dearest friends. You owe it to your partner. You owe it to your children. You owe it to yourself most of all. Showing up means you keep going even when it's hard—not because you want to but because you must.

I know it's hard, and I know you're hurting, but the pain that you're in will not get better unless you fight to make it so! One step at a time—that's all I'm asking. Showing up for others takes you out of yourself too! It forces you to think of something and someone besides the pain that you're experiencing. So, get up, take a shower, take a walk. Put one foot in front of the other. One hour at a time. Show up, do it for the people you love most. Because you can, and because you have to. The tiny steps you're taking today will become strides tomorrow and eventually become a new pace and a new cadence for your life.

Yes. You can and you *must*. Show up.

## THINGS THAT HELPED ME

**GET THE KIND OF HELP THAT YOU NEED:** Every single one of us manages stress in different ways based on tons of different factors. If you're struggling to continue to show up the way you want to then it's highly possible you haven't found the kind of help that you need. My sister joined different groups for widows when she lost her husband because she found solidarity in their stories and purpose in being able to help others who were going through something similar.

For me? When I go through something hard, I am deeply private about it. I would never feel comfortable processing things in a group. Neither one of us is doing it the right or wrong way, because when it comes to grief there is only *your way*. You have to figure out what will work best for you even if doesn't make sense to others. Just remember, *processing* grief is an action you take, not a destination you stay in, unmoving.

**NEVER LET THEM SEE YOU RUN:** This sounds like a random directive, I know, but let me explain . . . Back when I first started in business, I was a wedding planner. Over the years as I built up my reputation and my standards for my team, I started to develop rules for every event that we produced and the first one was, never let them see you run. I always told my team, "No matter what is happening, never let guests see you running." Because think about it: if you're at a beautiful wedding and all of the sudden you see the staff sprinting somewhere, your natural instinct is to believe something is wrong. Our job as event planners was to ensure that everyone felt comfortable and safe and had a great time, and the way to ensure that was to create an atmosphere in which we were calm and centered at all times. Over the years I had every—and I do mean every—terrible disaster that could possibly happen at an event happen, and no matter what, we always stayed calm and handled it in a way that ensured the guests never knew a thing was amiss. I take on this same belief when it comes to being present during hardships and still managing everyday life. Your children should not know that you are stressed out. If you're worried, you need to protect them from that. If you're having a hard day, go into your room and have a good cry or a glass of wine or scream into a pillow. If you are grieving, still make the pancakes. Do not let your kids see that you're struggling. I know a lot of people will

disagree with me on this, but I don't care one bit.
It is not your children's job to take care of you.
It's okay for you to be anxious, it's okay to be
afraid, but your job as a leader in your family, your
community, or on your team is to create stability
for the people in your care and that's impossible if
they're worried about you not being okay.

### BE FANATICAL ABOUT MANAGING YOUR STRESS:

The reason I'm so obsessed with talking about
creating habits to help you manage everyday stress
is because of how much those rituals will serve
you when you're managing something far more
drastic. You must be fanatical about developing
daily habits that will allow you calm space so
you don't take it out on your family. One of the
most important pieces of advice that I can give
you about showing up well for your family is that
you have to take care of yourself first. I know it's
easier in times of crisis to worry about everybody
else and make sure that they're okay, but you can't
pour from an empty cup. The kind of self-care I
am fanatical about, and you probably know this,

is moving your body every day, staying hydrated, eating foods that are good for you, taking your supplements, spending time away from social media, talking to a therapist, and most important, getting some freaking sleep! Take care of yourself today so you can be stronger tomorrow.

# 8

## GET REAL ABOUT YOUR FINANCES

Eighteen days after my brother died, we got a bill from his dentist.

It's one of the ugliest things I can remember from that time because it just seemed so incredibly insensitive. It arrived in the mail just two and a half weeks after his funeral—a time period that will forever remain in my memory as hazy at best. In fact, in the murkiness of that season this is the only thing I remember. My dad opened a bill for Ryan's wisdom teeth surgery, something that had happened a couple of months before, and even though he was dead and that surgery wasn't doing anyone any good, the bill had to be paid.

"Why would they still make you pay for that?" I demanded. I thought it was so unfair of the dentist to ask for that money. We lived in a small enough town that he surely would have been aware that my brother had just died.

"The dentist did his work. He has bills too," my dad told me. "The show must go on." He has always dropped dramatic one-liners into conversations—a holdover from the years he spent in the pulpit. But this one I remember so distinctly because he seemed so weary he could barely hold his head up as he said it. He shook his head at the ground and then slowly walked away to make the first payment against the cost of an unnecessary surgery for a dead boy.

The show must go on.

During the quarantine we experienced from Covid-19, we small-business owners felt this keenly. Every single month that passed we sent a check for the rent on our new office space. I'd signed the lease in early March 2020 for a massive office that would hold our entire team of sixty in one space and gave us room to grow. Every single month I paid a ton of money for a building that sat empty, just like many of you did . . . the show must go on. And does, regardless of whether or not we have the ability to pay for the show in the first place.

This chapter is different from others in the book. But it feels important. I wrestled with how to fit it in because it is focused on such different information than what I normally share. And yet, if you've ever gone through a crisis or are going through one now, then you know that money, and more specifically, your personal finances, has the ability to make what you're going through either a little bit easier or even more debilitating. I am speaking as someone who has lived in extreme financial insecurity as a child and as an adult. I am speaking as someone who has achieved financial security in my late thirties. I am deeply aware of the disparity between the two. I am also hyperaware that my audience is predominantly women, and women are the ones most at risk of financial instability inside of a crisis. We don't talk about our financial realities enough before crisis and we sure as hell don't explain to women how to handle their money if they find themselves in a time of upheaval.

So, we're going to have a chat. We're going to talk about hard seasons and money for a minute and if thinking about *your financial situation* makes you want to quit reading right now, fight that urge, you need this conversation the most!

Let me be crystal clear with you right now—you

need to get your money right, no matter what happened to you. Financial freedom, however that looks, gives you space to heal and grow. Financial fear is a prison that many people will spend their whole lives locked inside of, not realizing that they are the ones who hold the keys.

First, you need to do an assessment of where things stand. No guessing, no estimating, no assuming. If you can't see the evidence in a bank statement or retirement funds, it isn't real. Have the courage to look because I swear to you, we can solve *any* problem if we can see it. The things that truly tear us apart are the things we ignored until it was too late.

You need to see things as they are. Not better than they are, not worse than they are, but rationally and realistically so you know how to take care of yourself and the people you care about. When the Covid-19 virus began to make inroads into the U.S., and I started to realize what it would mean for our business, I had to fight the urge to panic. I spent a full week with my leadership team, like many business owners did, trying to determine what to do when there were no answers. We had to make a lot of difficult decisions and we had to make them quickly—and the majority of those decisions were Band-Aids. They were quick fixes to cover a hundred tiny leaks in a dam that felt like it might give way at any moment. A large majority of our company revenue comes from live events, and suddenly live events could no longer happen safely, and not only that, nobody knew when they'd be able to happen again. That revenue plays a big part in supporting the overhead for our team at Hollis Company—the sixty amazing people who work with me at HQ in Austin, Texas. That's sixty people with bills and car payments and groceries. Many of them have children, most of them have student loans, all of them were counting on their paycheck continuing to clear.

I am proud of how conservative we are when it comes to business finances and savings, but I've been an entrepreneur for seventeen years now. I've taken my company through business downturns. Through a recession. I know how fast you can burn through resources when the revenue flow stops.

The show must go on.

At Hollis Company, we immediately cut every single unnecessary expense from our books. We froze any projects that we could and put a hold on our hiring process even though we were in the midst of filling multiple open positions. What I saw was that we were okay, but that if things in the economy continued to get worse, we wouldn't be okay in a handful of months.

What this looks like in your personal life is being honest about where you are financially. If you're doing great, ask yourself what would happen if you lost your job and didn't have your regular income for nine months. Once upon a time the idea of that seemed inconceivable to many people—yet as I write this sentence over 30 million Americans are on unemployment. Look at where you're at financially and have a plan for what to do if it gets worse. If in any way your finances feel unsteady, it's time to go Edward Scissorhands on your expenses. Get rid of everything that isn't a necessity. A home, food, water— those are necessities. Your iPhone, Netflix subscription, trips to Starbucks—those are luxuries. I know it sucks to give them up—I've done it many times. But you know what sucks more? Truly getting to a desperate financial place because you didn't want to give up your access to Instagram. Remind yourself that this isn't forever and it's so much better to make this choice yourself rather than have your circumstances make it for you. David Bach was on my podcast not long after everything shifted for our business and he gave listeners such a great piece of advice about slashing your budget. He said that if you struggle to know which things to cut you should ask a friend to look your budget over for you. Our friends are way better at calling us out on unnecessary spending, because there's nothing emotional tied to any of those things for them. As daunting as this might seem, the simple act of taking charge of what's going on with your money and being proactive about a solution, or creating a cushion, will give you an incredible sense of control.

Often, a loss in your life is tied to a loss in income. Seeing someone through a long illness can mean massive medical bills. A loss of a job means that you need to seek out other ways to earn money. A divorce means that what was a single family with one set of bills becomes two, and often, a complex set of financial arrangements around children and spousal support. The worst thing you could do when faced with these life changes is focus on what is lacking financially. Said another way, focus on what is in your control, what you can affect, what you do have instead of obsessing over all that you don't. It's incredibly easy to spiral into thinking of all the things that could possibly go wrong because of money.

Because you're focused on what could possibly go wrong, you become paralyzed—or worse, you lie to yourself and pretend something is true that just isn't.

In the midst of all these changes at Hollis Company I started to reach out to other business owners I knew, and I was shocked at the number of people who were utterly in denial. I am devastated because those same people who didn't truly see things as they were, meaning they didn't see what was happening in the market or didn't understand what their finances could handle, continued to function as if we were living in business as usual. They didn't see things as they were, they saw them as they *wanted them to be.* They made things up that weren't really there. They counted on things that might happen instead of being realistic. In the end, their unwillingness to face reality cost many of them their businesses and countless people their jobs.

I know what it means to have to make hard decisions for yourself and your family. I know what it means to have to lay people off. I know what it means to have to downsize, to have to give up the office and go back to working out of my garage. And I know what it means to have built up to a certain place and suddenly feel like you've lost all the traction you worked so hard for. And,

I know that in the face of loss, the pain becomes greater when you also lose the ability to provide the most basic needs for yourself and your loved ones.

There's a book that I have loved for years called *The Hard Thing About Hard Things* by Ben Horowitz. In it he includes this line that is so fantastic I have to share it. He writes, *"If you have to eat shit, don't nibble."* Meaning, in the context of this conversation, if you're going to have to make some hard financial decisions don't play at it. Don't tiptoe around and try little tiny changes hoping they will make a big difference. Don't nibble at the problem, take a big ol' bite and deal with the crap all at once. Do what you need to do to be financially stable. Do what you need to do to be strong for yourself.

In 2008 I owned a high-end event planning company in Los Angeles, and if you're not familiar with that particular year in American history then I can tell you, it was an economic dumpster fire. If you're wondering what kind of interest there was to hire event planners in 2008 and 2009, there *wasn't*. Nobody was asking me to plan events and all of those I had booked in advance were canceled because of loss of funding. I had no idea what to do but I had a staff and a family counting on me. I needed to make money. It wasn't an option for me to give up. I'd worked too hard to go down without a fight. And you know what I'm guessing? *You've* worked too hard to go down without a fight too.

The show must go on.

If you're in a similar situation to what I was all those years ago then you're going to have to do exactly what I did then and in this more recent financial crisis. Back then, just as now, I looked at where we really were. I got rid of any expenses that were nonessential. I figured out every way I could think of to make extra revenue for my business without spending money to do so, and then I worked like the devil was on my heels for the better part of twenty-two months until the economy and my business were stable and safe again.

How did I continue to make money in a world that no longer wanted to hire event planners? First, I figured out who absolutely had to have events and they became my new favorite customers. Before everything went south my business had been primarily supported by large-scale corporate events for the entertainment industry but those were instantly gone. But there were some businesses that still needed events and I fought tooth and nail to land them as customers. Weddings still happened even if they weren't on the same scale as before—I leaned heavily into wedding planning even though I honestly hated the work because most brides in Los Angeles were awful. I know that's a sweeping generalization, but I've planned hundreds of weddings and can count on fewer than two hands the brides who were actually nice. Unfortunately, "decent human being" was not a requirement for my clients during that time—the only thing required was the budget to afford my company and keep my team in their jobs. The companies that still *needed* events were nonprofits since many of them used their annual gala as the fundraiser that would keep them in business. I learned everything I could about fundraising and silent auctions and turned that into a new line of business for us too. The irony of course is that both the wedding planning and my work in the nonprofit sector ended up becoming the bedrock of my business long after the economy was healthy again. It's a truth that the things we build in times of crisis are often the sturdiest, because your desperation gives you clarity. All artifice is ripped away. All ego is gone. When survival is the only focus everything becomes very clear.

Do you need to find some additional revenue for yourself or your family so that you feel more stable about your finances? There is no shame in working two jobs. But there should absolutely be shame in slowly drowning while pretending that life is fine just so none of your "friends" know that you're struggling financially. I worked three jobs when I moved away from home because I knew I'd rather be broke and working three jobs then stuck inside of the life I'd come from. Better broke and free to live an authentic life.

Get a job if you need to. Sell your old stuff on eBay. Learn all about "flipping" things on Amazon and then go and do it. Go research, hit up Google, ask YouTube to help. If you're not sure how to make extra income there are so many ideas to help you but please remember this important prerequisite: figure out a way to make more income *that doesn't cost you any money to start.* For real. I'm positive someone is going to read this and be inspired to head on over to the Internet and ask how she should make extra income and then, four weeks later, her starter kit has arrived for the new at-home business she just paid $700 to join. Don't be dumb! Figure out ways to make money that don't require money. The easiest way to do that is a job that trades your skills in exchange for cash. Can you tutor? Babysit? Clean houses? Detail cars?

Do estate planning? Taxes? Do you still have your massage therapy license? What are you good at doing and/or know how to do that you could use to make money? If you really feel like starting your own business or side hustle is the answer, that's awesome—but be creative and smart. You can make money without touching your existing funds.

Look, I'll tell you right now, I don't care how much of a name I've built up for myself. If for some reason all of it was taken away and all of my savings were gone and I couldn't earn money the way I do now, you'd find me waiting tables or working at Starbucks or bagging groceries (and possibly all three) before I'd *ever* allow my family to suffer because of my financial situation. I wouldn't be embarrassed for a single second that my life looked different now. I'd be grateful as hell that I had some means to take care of us. There is integrity to an honest job well done and an incredible sense of purpose in taking back control over your finances and your life, even if it's one paycheck at a time.

Faking stability you don't have keeps you from achieving it. And struggling financially will always, *always* take up the space you need for healing.

## THINGS THAT HELPED ME

**FINANCES CAN BE LEARNED:** Nobody, and I mean nobody, comes into the world with the intricacies of personal finance as part of their being. When you're born the doctor checks you over and announces, *It's a boy,* or, if you're truly blessed, *It's a girl!* But never one time in the history of the world has a baby emerged from the birth canal and had a doctor declare, *It's an actuary!* Nobody, including Warren Buffett and Janet Yellen, ever came into the world with financial wisdom, and you know what that means? It means they had to learn all that they know! If the smartest financial minds on earth had to come by their knowledge through education, that means that you and I can do the same. You have learned thousands of things over the course of your life and managing your finances is one more that you can add to the list.

**UNDERSTAND YOUR FINANCIAL PERSPECTIVE:** Remember when we talked about how our past shapes our current perspective? Well, if you have negative feelings around money or personal finances it will be very powerful to ask yourself why. What is it about your past that has made you feel this way? What were you raised to believe about money and how is it affecting the way you look at it in your present? My parents had wildly diverging viewpoints when it came to money and finances, and the resulting strife in their marriage made me believe that debt was something to be ignored if at all possible. That belief meant that I spent many years ignoring both my personal and business finances, which caused me far more pain than if I had just had the courage to face them and figure them out. By understanding why I behaved the way I did with money I was able to catch myself whenever I was inclined to avoid my financial reality, which has saved me time and again in the years since.

*GET GUIDANCE:* If you weren't raised to have a healthy relationship with money then it will likely be helpful for you to have some guidance with where to begin. There are countless advisors and teachers on this subject and so many ways to go about it, but I have always thought that Dave Ramsey and his team are an incredible resource, especially if you're a newbie. Between the Ramsey Solutions' countless teachers, podcasts, and books there are a ton of resources available and many of them are free to consume. I appreciate their style because it's simple to understand (for both personal and business finances) and quick to produce results.

WHAT TO DO

# FOREVER

# 9

## BE SURPRISED BY RESILIENCE

The first time I gave birth it decimated me.

Yes, *decimate;* that is how I would most accurately describe my physical and spiritual being after the birth of my first son. My entire body felt like a wet cloth that had been rung out repeatedly in the hands of an angry giant. And if that isn't descriptive enough for you, let me be clear about my body postpartum—when I say *cloth* I don't mean a plush new face towel from Bed, Bath & Beyond . . . I mean an old T-shirt turned household rag that someone used to clean between the grooves in the minivan's hubcaps *and* remove the dead cicadas out of the front bumper *and* then didn't hang it up properly so now not only is it covered with various stains of indeterminate origin—it also smells vaguely of mildew.

Meeting my son and having him officially join our family? That was incredibly precious, but I would be lying if I said that every part of the experience was positive. The adjustment of becoming a parent, mixed with the pain my body was in after a difficult labor, made even simple tasks seem impossible. It took me months and months to feel like myself again and when I think back on it now, it seems like the foundation of who I was as a person got pulled out from underneath me. I had to rebuild this new version of myself piece by piece. I'm sure there are women and men who become parents and have a much easier time of it but for me, it took quite a while to find my footing with my first baby.

With my second baby, the physical bounce back was much faster. I don't know if it's because I knew what to anticipate going in, so even though what happened to my body was similar, there wasn't the psychological toll of the unexpected added in. Physically I healed in a quarter of the time with my second son . . . emotionally, that time was much more difficult. I had terrible postpartum depression and my second son was a much more difficult baby. I also had the added layer of a two-year-old to care for simultaneously. It seemed like the only thing I did was breastfeed and change diapers—I wasn't a person anymore; I was the food supply and the caretaker. I spent most of every day vacillating between being a zombie with no emotions and someone who couldn't stop crying. I daydreamed constantly about running away from home. *I could do it,* I thought to myself, *I should get in my car and drive away, they'd all be better off without me here.* It took a lot of help from my doctor and my husband and a lot of therapy to navigate out of that season and feel like myself again, but ultimately, I came out the other side and found strength I thought I had lost.

Then there was my third son. I often joke with other parents that going from one to two kids feels impossible but any additions after that are just par for the course. Your life is already wild and unpredictable so what's one more addition to the party? Having my third son was my easiest postpartum experience both physically and emotionally. I knew what to expect, I felt like a seasoned pro at how to care for him and myself, and I fell back into my routine quickly. Why? Because every time I went through labor, delivery, and life with a newborn I learned more, I got stronger, and I had more knowledge at my disposal.

What in the world do my postpartum experiences have to do with teaching you about resilience?

Everything.

Being resilient means you are able to withstand or recover quickly from difficult conditions. And in a season of hardship, or the seasons that follow, what we want so desperately is to have the resilience necessary to withstand the pain and grief and stress so that we're able to rise back up and keep going. I want to talk about the different ways that resilience manifests for us but before we dig into that I think we have to explain what makes you resilient in the first place. It's all well and good to discuss what resilience is and why it's such a powerful characteristic to build in yourself, but it doesn't do you any good if you don't know how to acquire it.

The reason I told y'all the story of each birth of my sons is because I hoped to illustrate for you that intentionally taking steps to move through difficult things is what gave me the resilience to withstand the next hardship set before me. While none of my children's births was without difficulty or both physical and emotional pain, all of them made me stronger for what came next. Every single instance when I did my best to keep going despite the hardship, I was learning the skills and gaining the strength to move through motherhood with more ease the next time. Learning how to soothe a crying baby, learning how to watch for their hunger cues, learning to listen to my own body when I needed rest instead of rushing to get the house clean in the hour the baby would sleep. Being kind to myself and allowing that postpartum sadness didn't make me a bad mother or person. These are things I learned with each baby and took with me into the next experience—because I needed that knowledge.

The truth is, if I hadn't gone through everything I did with my boys, there's no way I would have had the emotional capability to stay upright through the adoption process with my daughter, Noah. Had we not had so many failed adoptions before we were chosen by her first-mama (what we call her biological mother) I can't imagine making it through the emotional turmoil of those days in the hospital waiting to find out if she would truly be ours forever. But even more powerful than the strength I earned through resilience in that long and hard (but ultimately beautiful) process is the person I became because of needing that resilience in the first place.

Adoption is one of the most beautiful and most awful things in the whole world because in order for us as adoptive parents to have our daughter, another woman had to make one of the bravest, hardest choices in her life and give up her baby. It felt so terrible to hope for a decision that we knew would deeply hurt the person making it. Even three years later I am astounded by Noah's first-mama and the resilience she had, even at such a young age, to choose as she did. One weekend while I was writing this book was both Mother's Day and National Birth Mother's Day. If you're not familiar, the Saturday before Mother's Day is a day of awareness for women who have given up their babies for adoption. I think it's a beautiful idea, but I personally don't celebrate it. I honor Noah's first-mom on Mother's Day right along with my own celebration. I sent her some just-for-her pictures along with a note wishing her a beautiful day. While it would be easy for her to find thousands of shots of our daughter on my social feeds, I always make sure to send her photos that nobody else gets to see. On this Mother's Day and every other I told her that we love her and were celebrating her today too and that I will never stop being grateful that she chose me to be Noah's forever mom.

The irony about all of this is that when we started our adoption journey years before Noah joined our family, we were actively pursuing a closed international adoption, and later, when that failed, we chose a closed adoption through foster care. A closed adoption is one where you sever all contact with your child's birth parents and family. At the time, we told ourselves that was best for the child, but the reality is that it's the solution that made the most sense to our egos. We hadn't begun to truly navigate the world of adoption and foster care, so we had no real frame of reference. We would spend the next four years taking the countless parenting classes and home studies required for the adoption process. In those years I would have the opportunity to visit orphanages in other countries and group homes here in the U.S. We would spend an arduous season as foster parents and have a stark look at the brokenness of that system. We watched the most vulnerable, the children, be the ones most hurt by that complex machine. Along the way we learned so many things about life and people and the human spirit. We also gained a greater awareness of how to help an adopted child feel the most secure in who they are. The work we did over those years, the resilience we built up, changed everything about the relationship we would eventually have with our daughter and her biological family.

Years later, when we had our initial call with Noah's first-mom, I spent the entirety of our forty minutes on the phone talking about our favorite books—I never one time asked her for information about the baby. I made that conscious choice because I had years of experience and work under my belt and so, by that point, I understood that often birth moms are disregarded by adoptive parents even if it's unintentional. The excited perspective parents are laser focused on the baby and sometimes only interested in the woman carrying that child in relation to her ability to get the baby into the world in a healthy way. I'm sure you can imagine how disheartening that is to someone who is trying to decide how to choose another person to raise the baby inside of her. I never, ever wanted Noah's first-mom to believe that we cared more about the baby than we did about her. I promised myself (though it was an emotional roller coaster for me) that I would treat her like a young woman in our church who was having a baby and needed support and friendship. I promised myself that if she chose to keep her daughter that I would be happy for her even though it would devastate me. The decision to make the experience about Noah's first-mom, instead of the baby, helped me so much because even after Noah was born, I never once assumed that we would instantly take on any parenting role until she asked us to.

We deferred to her on everything and spent three days in a hospital in Omaha watching old movies with her while waiting the required time period for her to make a decision.

When the lawyer came out to the lobby to find us where we'd been waiting those last few hours, I was so emotional I could hardly hold myself upright. When she told us that we were officially Noah's parents, my legs gave out and I fell to the floor. All those years of waiting and hoping and dreaming and we *finally* had our daughter. Many of my readers have heard this story before but what you likely don't know is that just a few days later we were together with Noah's biological family for a big dinner and an extended meet and greet. Maybe you don't know that when Noah turned one year old we flew her first-mom out to stay with us for the party and when that baby saw her mom she squealed with her arms in the air and went toddling toward her as fast as her chubby thighs could carry her. I *swear* to you that Noah knew her. Since then there have been untold pictures and videos and notes. Since then there have been texts back and forth asking about family history of allergies or whether or not Noah's other siblings ever get heat rash when they have too much sun. I can't imagine a world where we don't have this re-lationship with a woman who has given us something so precious. While I know this kind of relationship isn't pos-sible with every adoption, I don't want to think of a reality where Noah wouldn't ever get to know her people—the ones who gave her perfect blue eyes, her irrepressible curls, and her sassy personality. Actually, that's not true. I *can* imagine that world. I can imagine a version of myself that would have made those decisions and felt justified in allowing my fear of the unknown to destroy my daugh-ter's ability to know her own story. And I know it would have been a horrible loss for Noah, and for us.

What I can see so clearly now in hindsight is how necessary all the hardship was. I honestly believe I needed to be tossed about in the waves for years, I needed it to last as long as it did. I needed that outer layer scraped off. I needed to become a more raw, more compassionate, more gentle version of myself. I needed to develop empathy around a hundred different adoptive stories I'd learned in that time to see that nothing about the process, or any of the parties involved, is ever as simple as good or bad, right or wrong, better or worse parents. I needed to go through all of the hardships of parenting over many years with many different scenarios so when the time came I could understand that it wasn't enough for me to accept another woman's child as my own—I needed to become a woman who would see *the child's mother* as someone who needed a mother's love and understanding and inclusion as well. I think that's the most surprising part about true resilience. Resilience makes you strong, and while you earn the right to your strength, you simultaneously become more tender. While you harness the ability to rise quickly from the ground, you don't fear the fall as much the next time. Resilience can only come from experience, and God willing, you're gaining wisdom from each and every lesson.

I do believe there are lessons in everything we walk through. I believe that we will either be made better by our trials, our losses, our tragedies, or we will be made worse; there is no in between. Do you want to be made into a better version of yourself because of your dark season, or do you want to come through as a shell of who you were? Only one person can make that decision for you. If you make the choice to embrace resilience, you will be amazed at the way it strengthens your soul and opens your heart at the same time.

## THINGS THAT HELPED ME

**BE HONEST WITH YOURSELF ABOUT WHERE YOU ARE:**
Take inventory of yourself and dive in deep. So
often pain and hardship can feel like one big
emotion when in reality it's a complex system of
many different feelings and some are much more
painful than others. The easiest way I know of to
do this is with a therapist but if that's not readily
available to you, journaling is an incredible way
to reveal to yourself what's really going on. If you
can be honest with yourself about where you are,
you'll understand if whatever you've gone through
is turning you into someone better or someone you
don't want to become.

**LOOK AT YOUR SCARS, NOT YOUR OPEN WOUNDS:** I
spoke about this in the opening of the book and I
can't think of a better way to explain it. If you want
to see how you have learned from the past and how
even hard things have made you better—if you
want to believe that's true—then look farther back.
Oftentimes, when I teach about the idea that this
hardship can be *for you* instead of something that's

happening *to you* people will try and mine their current hardship for lessons. That is infinitely more difficult to do because that current pain (the open, more recent wound) is still bleeding. It's far easier to look at older things (the scars that have healed over) and ask yourself questions like: Did that hardship make me better in any way? Am I more empathetic? Do I stick up for myself more because of it? Spend time marinating in all the ways that your pain has helped you and you'll begin to see new ideas. It's amazing to me that the hard times in my life that I've already mined for goodness still reveal themselves in different ways. Like, I'll meet someone who is struggling with a very similar situation to one I've gone through, and I'm able to speak to their exact struggle and offer some insight. Once again, that scar of mine is still showing up in good ways.

*IMAGINE THE ANTIHERO:* This might sound a bit unexpected coming from someone who is so die-hard about you imagining again and again how the best version of you would handle something difficult. But if that isn't working for you, maybe it would be more powerful to imagine what you ***don't*** want to become. Consider what the future looks like for you if you stay on the path you're on and don't make any changes. What kind of person will you be if you allow this bitterness or grief to slowly eat away at you? What will happen if anger or even rage is allowed to continue to rule you? So much of the person I am today is not because of the positive role models I had growing up but rather the number of examples of who I did not want to become.

# 10

## CLING TO YOUR GOOD HABITS, OR MAKE SOME NEW ONES

Raise your hand if you make bad decisions about food, alcohol, cigarettes, or other negative coping mechanisms when you're faced with something hard. I assume that's most people. Under a regular amount of stress, it feels hard to keep making good choices—but under *extreme* stress it feels almost impossible. Most people assume that this happens because eating that food or drinking too much wine is a comfort. In hard times those are things you can access easily, and they will make you feel better, for at least a little while. Although the close correlation between our coping mechanism and comfort is certainly true, that's not the full picture of why we struggle so much with seeking comfort in unhealthy habits. There's an actual scientific reason why we begin making terrible decisions for ourselves and seem incapable of getting back on track in times of trouble. Not everyone is even aware of that. Maybe you're one of those people who struggles with "willpower," always blaming yourself for not being stronger. That self-recrimination will inevitably lead to shame if it didn't start there to begin with.

*"I should be able to stop binge eating . . ."*

*"Why aren't I as strong as my sister, she never struggles like this . . ."*

*"I thought I was past all this . . ."*

*"I can't believe I'm back here again . . ."*

Those thoughts continue to swirl in our heads, which only makes us feel worse and often triggers us to go right back into the bad decision we're ashamed about. I can't tell you the number of times in my life I ended up stressed and binge eating half my pantry late at night. The binging made me feel deeply ashamed before I'd even left the kitchen. That shame always led me to think, *"What's the difference now? May as well just eat everything."* And then I did. I ate until I would make myself sick during more hard seasons than I can count. It was a vicious and awful cycle that I know many of you find yourself in occasionally or even regularly.

Listen up!

There's a reason this is happening, and it has nothing to do with your willpower. Not only that, but there's a way to circumnavigate it, and it all starts with habits.

I have spent the last four years of my life talking, teaching, and writing about habits in some form or fashion. I worry sometimes that I've talked about them so much that it becomes white noise for my readers. I worry that because you know that you *should* have good habits you may dismiss learning more about them or be unwilling to dig deeper on the topic because you feel like you already understand what the lesson is all about. Basically, I'm worried that you guys will start to think about developing good habits the way I think about flossing. I know I need to spend more time on it but since it's not drastically affecting my everyday life, I'm way laxer than I should be. I'm going to ask you right now to fight the urge to assume you know all there is to know about this topic because in a season of intense change, the habits, rituals, and routines *that are ingrained* are what sustains you. It's why I fight so hard for people to build their lives around powerful habits: my Start Today brand is completely focused on habit building, our RISE Health brand is all about creating consistent routines for your health . . . every single thing we do at Hollis Company is based in some form or fashion around habits that will help you create the life you want. I'm most widely known as a motivational speaker or writer, but I don't love that moniker. Motivation is fleeting. Motivation is situational. If you look to me (or anyone else) as a resource to motivate you, you won't ever build true confidence in *yourself*. You'll trick yourself into believing that you need me or a podcast or a conference to make you feel like you can do it and it's just not true. I don't want to motivate you (though it's certainly a cool by-product of the work I do); what I want is to help you develop a way of living that is so routine for you that you don't need motivation. Think about it, do you need to motivate yourself to brush your teeth each day? Sure, yes, some of you do. My eleven-year-old acts like I've asked him to carry a refrigerator on his back up a steep incline every time I ask him to brush his chops. But besides Sawyer, and some people who have weird feelings about mouth sounds (*you know who you are*), most of us don't need motivation to do the everyday routines of our lives. The magic question, then, is how do you make the things you want to do or know are good for you that aren't part of your routine now—how do you make *those things* as habitual as teeth brushing? Well, I don't want to sound lame here, but I wrote all about this in my last book, *Girl, Stop Apologizing,* and I personally hate when authors repeat what they wrote last time and it's also not the point I want to make with this chapter. If you want to read about how to build great habits, grab that book from your library and dig in.

The point of this conversation is how important those good habits are when you're in a hard place. Your great habits and positive rituals are the anchor you need in the storm, not just because they're good for you but **because your brain isn't wired to handle intense discomfort and keep making good decisions**. Meaning, if you haven't already built your muscle memory for making consistent good choices, you'll find it nearly impossible to do so once life gets hard. On the same tip, we can also be anchored by terrible habits too and if you have a routine of drinking too much or grabbing a cigarette when you're stressed, it doesn't matter how badly you want to change or how motivated you are on New Year's Day, that bad habit will slip right back in the second your life goes off-center and you're not paying attention.

Okay, here's the deal . . . I'm about to nerd out on some science so I feel like it's important to note that I am obviously not a doctor. This is information I have because I've read a bajillion books on a subject that fascinates me—in this case, how the brain works. I'm going to describe this as I understand it but if it doesn't sound scholarly, well, you know why. The point isn't that this is eloquent, the hope is that you gain an understanding of why it is so hard to make good decisions in a difficult season.

Back in the 1960s a neuroscientist named Paul D. MacLean formulated a model for something called the Triune Brain theory. There's some debate over exactly how our brains evolved, but for explaining how each part of the brain *works,* there's no better reference that I know of. Feel free to go read up on it using all the scientific terms your heart can handle, but I'm going to explain it to you as simply as I can. The word *triune,* in case that's not a part of your current vocab, means three in one. It's most commonly used in reference to the Holy Trinity but for Dr. MacLean's purposes it referenced the idea that the brain could be divided into three sections. Before I carry on, please understand that I'm not suggesting that the human brain, one of the most elaborately intricate systems on earth, is simply three parts. The brain is utterly incredible and could never be categorized so simply. But for this particular model, there are three sections.

The first section is called the reptile brain, the second section the mammal brain, and the last and biggest section, we'll call that the human brain. The reason that each section has those names is that each section functions like that particular creature. For instance, the reptile brain (aka, the area around the base of your skull) controls your fight-or-flight response. This ability to react quickly was crucial eons ago when humans needed to be alert to constant threats. If a saber-toothed tiger rolls up, your lizard brain acts just like a lizard would if it sensed danger. If you walk out the door and a lizard is sitting on your front porch, it doesn't consider or think, the lizard just reacts. The reptile brain has one objective, *stay alive,* so the lizard doesn't wait to see if you are truly a threat, it just hightails it off that porch.

The second section of your brain is the mammal brain, so imagine that as a deer—or more specifically, imagine that as the kind of deer that hangs out in my yard here in Texas. The reptile brain controls your fight-or-flight response and wants you to stay alive at all costs, but the mammal brain (also known as the limbic brain) controls your emotions, memories, and habits. Think of it this way. If I walk out into my yard and a deer sees me, it has a more evolved thought pattern than a lizard might. It will sift back through memories and feel out the situation for long enough to make a decision. The deer in my yard in Texas? They've seen a lot of humans—many of which set up special deer feeders in their yards—so they're not afraid when they see me, they go right on chewing our grass. That wouldn't be the same response of a deer in the mountains in Oregon whose only experience with humans is one of fear because it's such a popular location for hunters. The point is that the "mammal brain" has a more complex thought process than the "lizard brain" does.

The last section of the brain is referred to as the human brain because it's where your rational thought lives. This is where things like language, imagination, and reasoning are stored. Scientifically this is known as the neocortex— the gray wrinkly outer layer that you picture when you think of the brain. The neocortex is the section of your brain that holds your lobes (there are four of them but I'm already going too deep on the science here, just stick with me, I swear there's a point). The neocortex houses your frontal and temporal lobes, which are the part of the brain most often damaged by a traumatic brain injury.

Have you ever known someone who suffers from a TBI? The symptoms are often directly related to the part of the brain that's been damaged. Impaired decision making, lack of impulse control, trouble concentrating—all are signs that the part of the brain that controls these things, the human brain, has been damaged. People with TBI can also struggle with aggression, depression, and personality changes, all of which are controlled by a specific area of our brains. Now, here's where stress and habits come into play.

When life is normal and good your human brain is in control. Everything works from the top down with your frontal lobe/human brain leading the way. You can make good decisions and focus well because there's nothing prohibiting that from happening. You can make the right decisions about your diet, your alcohol intake, how much social media to let yourself digest. But, in times of stress caused by grief, loss, or anything painful, your lizard brain/limbic brain freaks the hell out. The fight-or-flight response that has always been at the ready takes over. It's called an amygdala hijack, meaning, your amygdala (the part of your brain that processes anger, fear, sadness) literally hijacks your higher mental function. Instead of energy flowing down from the top, your brain begins to process from the bottom. In doing so, it drains the blood flow away from your frontal lobe down into the brain core and the rest of your body.

Okay, y'all, I know that was a lot of words and information you didn't ask me for, but do you understand what all this means?? It means that in times of extreme stress your rational mind, your ability to make decisions, everything that goes on in the "human" part" of your brain, is drastically impaired. It's why you're struggling to make good choices for yourself and it's also why it's utterly essential that if you want to live a life filled with things that are good for you—moving your body, staying hydrated, prayer and meditation, eating nutritious foods—then those good things (whatever they are) are going to have to be *ingrained*. In times of grief, crisis, loss, fear, pain, you aren't well capable of making good decisions, but instead fall back on whatever you *don't have to think about* because your brain function is impaired. Consider this: have you ever kicked a bad habit and given it up for a long time and then had a crisis happen and almost immediately you reach for the bad habit you haven't touched in years? This likely happened because that habit was the only one you had to draw on in times of extreme stress. Your mind latched onto only one thought, *Make this pain go away!* And so, you reached for something that you knew would alleviate it—a bad habit that didn't even require conscious thought.

I'm not obsessed with great-habit creation because those habits make the good days better (though that's an incredible added bonus). I'm obsessed with great-habit creation because they make the bad days bearable. As I type these words for you, I'm not sure if I've ever gone through any season as hard as this one that has also been so demanding on me professionally. Said another way, I've never been simultaneously physically, emotionally, and mentally drained, but for totally different reasons. I can understand that many people would say, *"You're going through a divorce, take some time off of work,"* but unfortunately, I'm going through the end of my marriage in the midst of a global pandemic and a despairing economy and massive societal change, and we are nowhere near the end of any of this. I have a team of people counting on me to be strong and keep leading well so that they still have jobs. I have children counting on me and my family counting on me and a series to finish shooting and this book to edit and a good example I am determined to set—which was all a buildup to tell you that as I type this sentence I'm eating an apple and raw almonds. Eight years ago, I got through much less intense times with vodka and fries and burritos the size of my forearm. I would stress eat and binge eat and drink too much because those were the only habits I had when life got hard. Last night during a difficult conversation with Dave, I closed my eyes and centered myself by breathing. This morning I woke up and worked out, like I do every single day. Today even in the midst of stress I reached for healthy things for my body, without conscious thought. I have changed my anchors, evolved my habits, and in so doing I have made the good days great and the bad days bearable instead of self-destructive.

Whatever hard thing you're going through, or will go through in the future, is already going to suck enough on its own—don't add to the pain by hurting your body, your mind, your soul, by reverting to bad habits.

### HABITS THAT HELP ME

PRAYER: I spend my days and sometimes many hours at night talking to God, talking to my guardian angels, talking to, honestly, anything that might be out in the ether listening. It helps me to think that my grandma or my big brother are with me in spirit and I sometimes feel their energy propping me up when I need it most. This season has reminded me that our prayers don't have to be eloquent so long as they're sincere and made with an open heart. The ritual of my faith has sustained me time and again through all the good and bad seasons of my life.

*INTUITIVE WORKOUTS*: Daily movement is a cornerstone in my life. I work out for at least thirty minutes every single day, only now—for the first time ever—I base my workout around what I *need* today instead of what I might normally do. In the beginning of this difficult time, there were days I'd go out to the garage gym and just stretch for half an hour or maybe take a very slow walk. Lots of days I've put on all my workout clothes only to go dance to music for a while. My heart and energy need this daily anchor in my life, but I just don't have the energy for my usual nine-mile runs or intense strength training. I'm sticking to my habit (same time every day) but I'm allowing it to be something new and different to meet me where I am.

**ALL THE THERAPY:** As you probably know by now, I am an enthusiastic proponent of therapy and have gone to see a counselor as needed for the better part of two decades. During quarantine, my therapy has to look different than it ever has before. Now I "attend" therapy sessions virtually and I do them in my car—I go sit in my car in the driveway or an empty parking lot so I can have my session without my kids overhearing or interrupting the conversation. Also, the drive home afterward is a helpful way to decompress or process what I just talked about.

## //

### *CHOOSE JOY EVEN WHEN LIFE SUCKS*

Long before I ever wrote a book or worked in personal development—long before there was social media or even the Internet—I laughed at funerals. My whole family does. In fact, some of the driest, most hilarious jokes I've ever heard in my life were graveside. If you think that's inappropriate or disrespectful, then my guess is you've lived a blessed life. Only people who've rarely encountered grief or hardship hold it at a distance. They believe that if they can separate themselves from those negative emotions fully after the initial experience, then perhaps it won't touch them again. Those of us who've lived through regular seasons of pain understand that there is no way to hide from it or escape it or circumnavigate around it. We know that when grief and pain show up in our lives—and of course they will—the only thing you can do is accept them, take whatever measure of comfort you can, and continue to live even in the wake of death. When Dave and I had been dating for a little over a year his grandfather passed away after a long and valiant fight with Parkinson's. His funeral, when it came, was somber but also a relief to a family who had watched their beloved patriarch slowly succumb to a horrible disease. When we were driving away from church Dave was in a bit of a daze as he casually mentioned, "I think this is maybe the second funeral I've ever been to . . . or perhaps the third." He tried to remember the losses in his mind while I sat there reeling, thinking, *This is only your second or third funeral?*

I couldn't believe what I was hearing. Because we only tend to see things through the lens of our own experience (perspective, remember?) it never even occurred to me that there were people in the world who'd never attended a funeral or had possibly only attended one or two. I had been to at least fifty funerals in my lifetime by that point . . . possibly more. Is that a lot? It never entered my consciousness as anything more than what my family did. I didn't need to contemplate the reasons—they were so obvious they never crossed my mind—but here they are:

*1.* I come from a big Irish/Scottish Okie family; our people go to funerals. Our families are big and usually encompass several generations and when people die, we show up . . . and we bring a casserole.

The saddest thing our family can imagine is a sparsely attended memorial service, which is why *everybody comes.* Are you a baby? You're attending the funeral. Are you a wiggly three-year-old who will have trouble sitting quietly during the eulogy? You're attending the funeral. Are you a ten-year-old who should under *no circumstances* have to walk by a casket holding the remains of your great-great-second-aunt twice removed? You are walking by that casket, son!

*2.* I'm a preacher's daughter and a preacher's granddaughter and in our church culture (Southern church culture) if you know someone who *knows someone* who died? You're showing up. You don't ever leave others to grieve alone. I attended my first open-casket funeral before I was a flower girl in my first wedding. I'm not saying that was everyone's normal, but it was certainly mine, and as odd as it might sound to you, there is some blessing in death having always been a part of my life.

Because here's a truth that you might not hear—or maybe don't want to believe is true: we will all die someday. It's the cost of living.

It's easier to take in the concept when you're attending the service of an older family member who has lived a good life. It's hard to accept when it's your seventeen-year-old brother or your friend's favorite cousin who was taken by cancer before her twelfth birthday. Those losses are horrific in their own way but even in the midst of them, those of us who'd experienced pain before them . . . even then, we fought for whatever joy we could find.

At my brother's funeral I remember sitting with my sisters cracking jokes about the menu options available to Ryan in heaven since he basically lived off Taco Bell and Top Ramen. I don't remember that what we said was especially funny, but I do remember laughing so hard we were crying . . . it was the first time we'd smiled since he died, and the catharsis of that moment is still with me twenty-three years later. When my brother-in-law Michael passed away unexpectedly last year our entire family mourned him keenly. He and my sister started dating when they were twelve and thirteen, so he was a part of our family for as long as I have memories. On the awful day when we gathered for his service, I linked arms with my big sister, prepared to walk her into the funeral of her childhood sweetheart and best friend. As we passed the hearse holding his casket I leaned over and asked, "Do you think we should crack a window so he doesn't get hot?" People around us were horrified, but Christina and I cackled like hyenas.

Have you ever heard of *gallows humor*? The first known use of the term was in 1901, as in, someone who was sentenced to death began cracking jokes along the way to the gallows, before they slipped the noose around his neck.

Dark stuff. I know.

The dictionary today describes the term as *grim and ironic humor in a desperate or hopeless situation.* There's also a place for joy even in the most hopeless of times . . . it's varying degrees of gallows humor and for me, it's always been the greatest testament left to those of us in the wake of tragedy. It feels a bit like thumbing my nose at the awful thing that's happening, like, *yes, okay, this situation is absolute garbage but damnit, **I'm still here!***

It might not *feel* appropriate for everyone—I wouldn't recommend cracking jokes at funerals in front of the wrong crowd—but I promise that fighting for a smile or some laughter when times are at their absolute worst will go a long way into making you feel strong enough to endure them. Who on earth talks about joy during a crisis? Someone who has been through enough crisis to know the power of a smile or a laugh.

Because even in the darkest times there are still reasons to smile and laugh. *Yes,* there are and yes, you can fight for those moments. And should. One of the beautiful things about being human is that we're capable of holding both joy and sadness simultaneously. Anyone who has ever raised a child through the toddler stage knows how true this statement is.

Have you ever had one of those days with a toddler? You know, one of *those days*? The kid is extra ornery and you're extra tired and everything seems like it's going from bad to worse and you haven't showered in two days and then . . . then that changeling that has inhabited the body of your formerly precious one-year-old, now with the spirit-testing antics of the terrible twos, then *that creature* finds a Sharpie. And to make this scenario worse the baby won't unleash destruction at any old moment.

No, sir. She'll wait until you've gone to do something supremely parental (like creating a little fruit plate for her where everything is cut to exacting standards to ensure that she won't choke) and then, *then* she'll go for total destruction. She'll take a Sharpie to the entirety of the sofa and she'll be absolutely sure and include the quilt that your grandma made you for your tenth birthday. For reasons both unfair and unholy, while she's adding more swirlies into the crack between the cushions she'll find a pair of safety scissors shoved there by her older brother. She'll use them to cut half the hair off her head—all the way to the skull, in some places, chunks of two- and three-inch patches in others. She'll get so excited about her sofa art and the confetti of soft baby curls she's created around her that she'll wet her pants for the first time in a month, and just when you thought the potty training had finally stuck and had bought her those big girl chonies with Elsa on them as a reward. This entire demonic process will take three minutes, tops. When you come around the corner holding her little fruit bowl shaped like Olaf and see the destruction that she's wrought to your couch, your beloved quilt, to her very own head, it will decimate your soul. Every parent has felt this kind of moment at least once. It's like a physical manifestation of all the ways you're failing as a mother right there in front of you covered in permanent marker. It will knock you to your knees. Or . . . you'll begin to laugh.

You'll begin to laugh the deepest, most cathartic—yes, slightly crazy but no one is there to see you—from the *depths of your being* kind of laughter. You'll laugh because if you don't laugh, you'll cry. You'll sob. You'll find it hilarious because you know that what has happened is awful, but you've had just as much awful as you can manage today. You'll cackle at the thought of trying to fix this demon spawn's hair, and whether you can get away with shaving your baby girl's head. You'll double over at the idea of having to buy a new couch because there is NO WAY that marker is coming out of those cushions. You'll fight for joy because on some primal level you understand that this isn't the first time it's been hard to be a mom, and it won't be the last. You know that you will cry more tears again later, so right now, in the depth of this moment you're going to *choose* to allow yourself to feel something positive and choose to fight for your perspective. Your baby isn't hurt. Her hair will grow back. A couch will still function as a couch even covered in marker, and your grandma would have loved this baby and found absolute delight in her artwork—she would have said it only made that quilt prettier.

See that? You can choose. It's a choice.

Some people are naturally joyful, others have to fight a bit harder for that outlook, but it *is possible* for each of us to reach for joy despite how we were raised to process hardship. It is possible to gain strength and even courage from the moments of levity you create for yourself, and even more, you should want those moments. Why? Because you're going to have to endure the hard thing either way. Robert Frost told us long ago, *the only way out **is through**.* You're going to have to walk through it regardless; why not find something to laugh about along the way? Laughing feels good.

## THINGS THAT HELPED ME

**START A DAILY GRATITUDE PRACTICE:** My sister Christina sent me a picture recently of a "gratitude journal" I had made for her for Christmas one year long ago. In sloppy handwriting I had written instructions on the inside cover of the Dollar Store notebook to "write down things every day that you are happy about and also thankful too."

I was twelve at the time. If you know my story at all, or that one of the brands I created is called Start Today, which began with a daily gratitude and goal-setting journal, then you can understand how wild it was for me to realize I had been encouraging women to do this thing I loved since I was a little girl. The presentation wasn't quite so refined back then, but the soul of the practice was the same. I'd like you to challenge yourself to make a list every single day of at least five things that you're grateful for, but here's the catch. They have to be things that have happened in the last twenty-four hours and they have to be little things. When I do this, I usually sit for a few moments and meditate on the day and then write down beautiful moments that I got to experience. I include things like when my seven-year-old told me a joke, my three-year-old knowing every word to the *Frozen 2* soundtrack, someone on my team at work growing by leaps and bounds, getting a letter in the mail from my friend Rosie. My gratitude list acts almost as a little diary of my life and requires me to spend the entire day looking for things to be grateful for. It pulls me into the present again and again and again. Through this act of seeking gratitude, my perception of the world around me is that life is full of good things—even in the bad times.

**MAKE A JOY LIST**: If level one is the gratitude practice, level two is the joy list. I was reading a book once and the author made a sort of passing remark about something, saying, "It feeds my soul . . . do you know what feeds yours?" And while she was focused on big picture kinds of things, such as her family or summer vacations, I immediately started to wonder about the little things that "fed me." You might have noticed that I teach a lot on finding joy and gratitude in "the "little things" and not the big stuff. That's because the big stuff, like marriage, kids, your home, is hard to come by but incredibly easy to take for granted. If you think or write down "I'm grateful for my home," it's easy to dismiss because you don't feel that, really. You live in your house every day without giving it much thought. But if you write down "I'm grateful for my bathtub and taking long bubble baths while listening to Fleetwood Mac," *that evokes a feeling*. Both descriptions are talking about the same place, home. But by focusing on specifics you can create a more intense sense of gratitude in re-creating that moment in your mind. When I read that book, I grabbed my notebook and started making a list. I challenged myself to come up with at least twenty things that fed my soul, that made me feel utterly, ridiculously happy and joyful. I refused to censor myself at all. So, when the idea of a heating pad and really soft sweatpants popped into my head, I added both items to my joy list because, you guys, both of those things DO bring me joy. My list includes harder to achieve items like "international travel," but almost everything else are things that can easily be incorporated into a regular week. Some items on my list are:

- A slow cup of coffee while looking at a view
- Laughing with my kids
- Talking to people about how to grow their business
- Long, multicourse delicious dinners with my friends
- Really soft sweatpants
- Hawaii
- Reading historical romance novels

I know creating a joy list in the midst of your hardest seasons can seem inconsequential, but the truth is, it's a powerful bastion against the toughest things. Human beings have an incredible ability to hold both joy and pain simultaneously; don't dismiss one simply because you feel the other.

**LITERALLY, SCHEDULE IN YOUR JOY:** The gratitude list is filled with things that make me happy but just writing them down isn't enough. The whole reason you create your list is so you can schedule those things into your week, or even better, into every single day. That's why it's essential to have easily achievable items on the list because if the only stuff that makes you happy is massive, expensive, and hard to access then you're putting a high price tag on your joy. Open your weekly calendar right now and ask yourself which things from your list you could do today. One of my favorite things is also the first on my list because it's readily on my mind and that's a "slow cup of coffee with a view." I love slowly sipping a cup of homemade coffee while looking at something pretty. If I'm on vacation that coffee break gets kicked into high gear because there is usually something beautiful to look at, but most of the time, it's a cup of Folgers and me staring into my backyard. It's a ritual I indulge in nearly every single day of my life. In fact, I wake up extra early just so I can have it. I got up at four-thirty in the morning to write this book just so my cup of coffee could still happen "slowly." If you schedule your joy into your day, you'll find that it becomes sacrosanct to you and you'll move heaven and earth to make sure it happens. The benefits to your overall wellness will be incredible.

## 12

### REIMAGINE YOUR FUTURE

Purpose is what so many people struggle with after their world has been flipped sideways. When it feels like everything in our lives has changed, the things that once mattered often don't seem important anymore.

It's this awful catch-22: you feel lost because you don't know where you're headed, but it seems impossible to decide on a destination when you're so lost. Whether your life changed in an instant or broke down over a long period of time—you've gone through something that put you in the place to learn how absolutely unclear your future is at any given moment. Since you can't possibly know what's coming next, and therefore feel out of control, there's an impulse to believe that nothing really matters anymore when your world falls apart. Like, *Why should I even bother when I don't know what tomorrow holds? If I don't know what tomorrow holds, then how can I make plans or have goals? Why waste my time?*

Before we jump into ideas on how you can reimagine a future for yourself inside of your new reality, I want to make sure you understand something important. It won't matter how good my ideas are for vision casting (and I assure you, I think they're pretty great) if you don't get on board with one extremely important notion.

You are struggling with the uncertainty of your world because whatever crisis you've gone through has made you realize—some of you for the first time ever—that you are not in control of life. During the quarantine in the spring of 2020 our city of Austin, Texas, declared a mandatory stay-at-home order. Probably the same thing happened where you live. Because we were nonessential workers, we weren't allowed to leave our house except to go to the grocery store or the pharmacy. When we did go out, we had to wear gloves and masks, and frankly, the anxiety of leaving the house and seeing our once bustling city look like a scene from a postapocalyptic young adult novel made Dave and me not want to leave at all. Before quarantine I got lulled into a false sense of control because I had freedom over my life and my daily routine. I could go to the grocery store or to my favorite coffee shop or on a dinner date with my friends whenever I wanted, and since I'm an adult and I'm privileged to live in a country that doesn't control my day-to-day life, nobody else had a say in what I did. But the truth is, we were never really in control because we are *never* truly in control of life. If you've ever lost a loved one without warning, then you know that you are not in control. If you've ever experienced getting laid off or losing your business despite the fact that you put your heart and soul into the effort, then you know that you are not in control. If a partner has ever cheated on you, or you've made a personal mistake that tore your foundations away or created a loss of love, then you know that you are not in control of the actions of others either. If you or someone you love has gotten gravely ill, then you understand that you are not in control.

We don't ever truly know what life is going to look like from one day to the next. Even from one hour to the next. We've never been able to accurately predict the future. I want you to understand that you haven't lost control of life . . . because *you never had control to begin with.*

What you *did* have was a false sense of security in

your own ability to control the world around you. When something happens to disturb that belief, when a crisis blasts that notion to hell in one fell swoop, the fallout can leave you shell-shocked and unable to move forward. The ground you thought was firm is suddenly unsteady. The dreams you thought were yours to grasp seem like just another disappointment waiting to lay you low. But even the belief that you've lost control during this change implies that your current reality, and the influence you have over it, was ever in your control to begin with. The state of unknown that you're currently residing in isn't new, **only your awareness of it is.**

And here's another hard truth . . . at some point in time you will forget that awareness again and you will go back to believing you have authority over what does and doesn't happen to you. You will subconsciously make this decision to back into that false state of security because the reality of uncertainty came from pain, and who wants to be constantly reminded of pain? I know this happens because even though I have lived much of my life in situations that were harsh and unfair and entirely out of my control, when a new crisis occurs I am still jolted by the reminder that I have only ever been in control of myself and my actions. I was never in control of the state of the world, only my response to it. I was never in control of my husband's life or the success of my marriage, only the role I would play inside of both.

We are only ever in control of ourselves and our actions in the moment. That statement holds utter limitation or ultimate opportunity, and the only thing that will decide which way it lands in your life is how you choose to view those words. Will you choose to look at your own abilities as the reason why you'll never get past this place you're in? Or will you decide that enough is enough? Will you decide that you don't want to keep living in your pain and your loss? Will you fight to hone the one great tool you actually have, which is yourself? Will you stop mourning for a future that was not yours to control anyway? If that's what you want to do, and I certainly hope it is, then these are the steps I have taken time and again to rebuild a new foundation for myself.

## THINGS THAT HELPED ME

**MAKE PEACE WITH THE UNKNOWN:** I need you to make peace with the fact that you do not know what the future is going to bring. This is not easy. The only way that you can make peace with an unknown future—which, P.S., is the only kind of future there has ever been—is to harness strength from your past and live wholly and fully in the present. If you've ever come to one of my RISE conferences, then you know that I spend a full day teaching on coming to terms with and finding power in your past. I do this because I believe that the obstacles we've overcome in our past don't make us weaker, I believe those trials make us warriors. Plenty of people will look at their past and only see the hardships, the hurt, the loss, but I choose to see all my pain and trauma and grief as the reason I am the woman I am today. When I am able to harness that strength and fight to stay present in the present, I don't need to worry about the future. I can rest in the knowledge that today is enough.

**MAKE A CONSCIOUS DECISION TO REBUILD:** When we come through crisis, we are forced to build new foundations. Whether you are aware of doing so or not, you are laying the groundwork for the life you will have from here on out. You are creating—

consciously or subconsciously—your new reality and if it must happen either way, then please, be conscious about what you are doing. The gift in this—yes, I said *gift*—is that you *are* able to rebuild and in doing so, you get to decide what is a *must* in your life and what you need to let go of. The hard part, I know, is that even if you rebuild your life and sense of self in the most thoughtful, intentional way it is still a difficult process. In fact, it might feel almost impossible at some moments in your journey. You will still feel sad. You will still cry for what or who you've lost. But dang it, if you're going to have to go through hell you should at least come out the other side with something to show for it! Don't just rush right back into life as it was, first ask yourself what isn't worth bringing forward with you.

**ASK YOURSELF HOW YOU CAN REBUILD BETTER THAN BEFORE:** Dave and I bought our first house many years ago, a tiny little Spanish-style bungalow in a suburb of Los Angeles. It was our first big purchase, so we didn't have a lot of funds. However, we really wanted to refresh the kitchen that hadn't been touched since the 1950s—our biggest goal was to put in a dishwasher and change out some cabinets. Unfortunately, old houses hide a lot of problems and the simple act of trying to install a dishwasher revealed that the plumbing was corroded and needed to be replaced. Not just in the kitchen either, but all throughout the house. What started as a small remodeling project turned into full-scale pandemonium, with holes in every wall in the house and a price tag we would spend the next year paying off. This was such a disappointment but complaining about the unfairness of it all wouldn't have changed things and ignoring the issue would have only led to bigger and more costly problems later. Once the pipes were replaced and the crew began to replace the drywall, I found a little ray of sunshine. We would need to repaint! We hadn't planned on painting for a while because the dishwasher had taken WAY bigger priority over the fact that the bathroom walls were bright pink. But since we had to rebuild the walls, I was able to rebuild the house in a way that was my ideal. I wouldn't have chosen the situation, but I found a way to make the best of it.

## WRITE DOWN YOUR VISION OF THE NEW YOU:

Hopefully those first few prompts have allowed you to begin to see a vision of the kind of future that feels like it's worth creating. Worth fighting for. If you need some help coming up with ideas then grab a notebook and try completing these prompts: *The things I love most about my life today are . . . If I could change anything about my life it would be . . .* In both instances I'm going to ask you to focus most on the present life you have and your future possibilities. If you write down what you wished *would have happened* or how you want things to be different, it won't serve you. Instead allow yourself to daydream about the possibility of what the new you can be. Be as specific as you can as you write. How would the *best version* of you take on the next four months? What would your days look like? Who will you spend time with? What great things were a part of your life before your hardship that you've begun to rebuild? What *isn't* a part of your life now because you were conscious about letting it go? Please don't second-guess yourself or try and talk yourself out of the ideas that come to you. Just write down anything that pops into your head. I ask you to do this because something powerful happens when we begin to articulate our daydreams. That's what you're doing now. It makes them crystallize in our minds and gives us something purposeful to move in the direction of. There's a good chance that one of the things that's causing you anxiety is that your mind keeps spinning around with thoughts of "*What now?*" or "*Will I ever be happy again?*" or "*Will I ever get over this?*" By creating a narrative for yourself that shows a beautiful vision of your future—even one that is different from what you were planning—you're answering those questions for yourself and quieting that noise in your mind. You're giving yourself direction and setting an intention, not to control every part of your life but with the understanding that you *are* in control of the way you move through it.

*CHOOSE ONE THING THAT YOU WILL STOP DOING IMMEDIATELY:* It's not enough to just be conscious of it, or even to write it down. Challenge yourself to first create, then really examine a list of things you won't bring into your future with you and choose one thing to stop doing immediately. Maybe you've just endured a terrible divorce after a marriage to someone who always belittled you, and you know that the thing you want to leave behind is not speaking up for yourself. Maybe you will decide today that you will stop staying silent; from this moment forward you will share your opinions regardless of how you think they'll be received. Maybe you fought for years to get your dream job and a shift in the economy brought everything you've worked for to a crashing halt. Perhaps the thing that you need to let go of is living for other people's opinions. Losing that job didn't make you less of a person, getting a promotion won't make you more of one. All of us have things that we desperately need to let go of; choose one today and instantly live in the power of that choice.

**CHOOSE ONE ACHIEVABLE GOAL THAT YOU WILL START PURSUING IMMEDIATELY:** Look, I get it, the very last thing most people want to think about in a difficult time is a goal that they can pursue. Some of you may feel like you've been in survival mode for so long that the idea of trying to achieve something feels downright cruel. But, y'all, I swear there is a method to this madness. In full transparency, I love setting goals. You probably know this if you've hung out with me for long (I did write an entire book about it, after all) but growth is one of my greatest core values. The only way I know of to actively pursue growth in my life is to set goals both personally and professionally so that I am forced to grow as a person in order for those goals to be made manifest. I challenge myself in this way as a leader, as a mother, and as a friend. I truly believe that we find purpose in creating traction against a goal we are trying to achieve, so long as the goal is something we care about. When I talk about this subject it sometimes rubs people the wrong way because they associate the word *goal* with the industries that have adopted it most. People think that a goal must be for financial gain or weight loss or a bigger promotion or a nicer car since those are the categories in which the term is most often used. But the truth is, a goal can be about anything. It doesn't have to be associated with what you've lost, what has caused you hurt. You can create a goal to show up as a better mother or to grow in your faith. You can create a goal to learn sign language or to pay off your student loans or to repaint your local community center. You can create a goal to learn to eat intuitively or to stop fighting with your sister. You could create a goal to learn to make the world's best carrot cake. It doesn't matter what the goal is, it only matters that you have one and that it's something you care about. Any area of your life that you feel passionately about can be improved upon by adding a specific goal to it, and the beauty is that you'll start to see the positive effects of your goal-setting long before you actually achieve anything. Once you start to see traction, once you start to see that you're truly making strides toward something you care about, you will find purpose not in the achievement but in the pursuit.

And when you actually do achieve the thing, the confidence it will give you in your ability to create the life you want is the foundation you'll use to propel you closer to that vision you created of the new you, the you who walked through the fire and came out scarred and beautiful.

*BELIEVE ME.*

## HOLD ON TO HOPE

Just when I think I've told you every story I have about the most traumatic part of my life, another bubbles to the surface. Big grief is funny like that. Just when you think you've got it completely in your grasp something comes at you and surprises you. This story is difficult for me to think on and also the greatest example I have of hope even in darkness. In order for me to tell you this memory you'll have to walk on a journey with me through the morning that my brother died. It won't be graphic but it's hard for me to write it out and it may be equally difficult for you to read it, but we can do that for each other, right? We can hold space for each other's pain and each other's joy and maybe find a lesson in it for our own lives as well.

I can't remember every single thing I've told you about that morning—I've written about it in three books now and talked about it onstage many times, so I can't quite recall what you might already know and what are my own shards of memory, but here it is, this version, in this way, for this purpose.

It was a Monday morning. September 29, to be exact. I was a month into my freshman year of high school and the awkwardness that had followed me throughout middle school was more evident than ever. I got up early that morning, something I never did back then but I wanted to *try*. I remember thinking that when I woke up. I remember thinking, *I want to try and fit in, I want to try and be popular, I want to at least try.* I'd never had any idea how to achieve those things but on that particular morning I decided that how I would try was that I would blow dry my hair. I was wearing a terry-cloth robe with rainbow stripes—something Aunt Linda had bought for me for $8 during one of her many Goodwill trips. I put my hair half up that day and curled the ends. I wanted to try eyeliner next, but I wasn't sure exactly how to apply it.

Then I heard the sound.

It didn't sound like a gunshot. It sounded like books falling off a high shelf and toppling to the floor. I laughed nervously at my reflection in the mirror.

I knew even then.

I didn't know what had happened—my brain kept telling me, *Ryan dropped a box of books*—but I remember laughing, I remember that it was forced. I remember putting down a blue eyeliner pencil and thinking, *I better make sure Ryan knows he needs to take me to school.* My parents were both at work by then and Ryan could drive; there was no question of whether or not he'd take me to school, because he always did. There was no reason to remind him. I wasn't even ready for school yet—I was still wearing that robe. But when something horrific happens your instinct senses it long before you do. My brain needed a reason to go into his room and that was the one it gave me.

I don't want to talk about what I saw; that shard of memory is mine to carry. I will tell you that I couldn't process what was in front of me. Everything was so wrong, but I didn't know why. I didn't scream and I didn't run out of the room. I walked over to him on legs that could barely move, and I reached out my hand. I can still see my fingers shaking violently as they reached out to touch first his throat and then sliding them to the side to feel for his pulse just like they taught us in health class. There wasn't one. It wasn't until I was that close to him that I saw the gun clutched in his hand.

My brain finally understood.

Then I did run out of the room. I ran all the way to the kitchen, where the phone was, and I called 911. I explained as best I could to the woman on the other end what had happened. I don't remember much of that conversation except for one single piece. I latched on to the same question and I screamed it again and again into the receiver.

"Is Ryan going to hell?" I sobbed to that stranger. "Is Ryan going to hell? Is he?!"

You have to understand, I was raised in an incredibly conservative Pentecostal church. I was raised to believe that if you died with unforgiven sins you went straight to hell. Since killing someone is a sin, the belief held by our church was that if you killed yourself you'd sinned, and since you couldn't ask for forgiveness afterward it didn't matter what kind of life you had lived before; you were doomed.

In what felt like hours but surely was minutes, police came and firemen and everyone rushed in and out of Ryan's bedroom in the back while I sat in the living room wearing my rainbow robe with my hair half up. One by one our family members arrived, and our house began to fill with people in various stages of shock and grief. My mema sat in the corner of the room weeping. "God forgive him," she wailed again and again. She was positive he had committed an unpardonable sin.

The whole day was a nightmare. The week that came after was filled with millions of painful moments that each cut in their own way. Calling to tell family and friends. Writing the obituary. My father explaining that he'd chosen a mint green casket because he didn't want Ryan buried in something dreary. Being afraid to sleep in my room because it was next to his. Worrying about my mom, who could barely function. Worrying about my dad, who I was positive would kill himself too. Worrying about my sister, who was pregnant at the time.

There was so much worry, too much, I can now see, for a child of fourteen to take on. Even when people asked how they could help or tried to offer condolences I had no idea what to say. In the midst of it all our house was overrun by casseroles and flowers and notes and visitors. All those funerals we'd faithfully attended over the years stood for something—over four hundred people came to Ryan's service, it was standing room only. I cannot possibly express to you how much this meant to our family—

how much it means to me still, all these years later. And then, a few days after the service, something even more meaningful happened. A card arrived in the mailbox along with the dozens of other condolences, but this one was addressed to me. No one recognized the name or the return address. When I opened it there was a handwritten note from the 911 operator who answered my call that day. She told me that she was so sorry about what had happened. She told me that I was brave and strong. She told me she wanted to make sure I knew, *for sure,* that Ryan was in heaven.

Until I read that note I hadn't remembered screaming that question again and again. This stranger gave me hope when I thought I'd lost it all. This stranger spoke truth into my life when I needed it most. I don't know that I'll ever do any work in my life as important as that 911 operator did by sending me that letter, but I do believe her willingness to reach out to a scared little girl is a big part of the healing that allows me to write these words down for you today.

This book is my attempt to write something similar to that letter. With a few lines she was able to shift my feelings on what had happened. With a few lines she gave me a truth that no one in my family would have dared believe—that the creator of the heavens and the earth is infinitely bigger and more loving than any religious dogma can contain. With a few lines she saw *my pain* and she made me believe that it mattered.

I see your pain.

I see how badly you were hurt. I see how desperately you want to feel hopeful. I see you—even in the midst of everyone else—because I have touched sorrow just like you have. I understand this is a club that none of us asked to join but we're here now, and we have to make it mean something. I refuse to believe we've walked through all of this because we're cursed. I can't believe we were made to suffer—I won't accept that that's why you are here. There is goodness in this world and there is light inside you still, even if it's been dimmed—even if others have tried to extinguish it completely.

I know you didn't plan to walk down this path but you're on it. I know if you've made it this far, you are strong enough to see it through.

You will get through this.

You will.

Humans can endure anything so long as they cling to

hope for what tomorrow will bring. My brother, and so many like him, isn't here to read these words because he lost hope. Years battling mental illness made him believe that life was hopeless and there is a huge part of me that is happy he doesn't have to endure one more second of that pain. But you know what?

He lost so much.

He lost hope and then he lost everything.

He lost out on a future that might have been . . . He lost the chance to meet his wife. He lost the moment when his son was born and two daughters after that. He lost the chance to dance with his sisters on their wedding days. He lost seventy-odd years of holidays and birthday parties and Fourth of July barbecues. He lost running his first marathon and ever going to a Dodgers game again. He lost out on wrinkles around his eyes and holding his grandbabies. He lost out on a whole beautiful life that could have been because he made a momentary decision that changed everything.

I'm telling you this now because some of you are making a decision every single day that is pushing away happiness, a future, that was meant to be yours. Not making a decision is a decision in itself. Not choosing to get help is *choosing* to stay stuck. Not standing back up is what is keeping you on the ground. I know it's hard and it's scary and maybe you're not sure what to do but I swear to you that life can be beautiful again. Good things will always be available to you if you look for them.

When we lost my brother-in-law Michael last year it was awful. He died unexpectedly of a heart attack that no one saw coming. And even though he didn't make the decision to leave us, the loss of what might have been was no less acute. I'm not telling you about these two brothers of mine to make you focus on death—I'm telling you these stories now so that you remember you still have a life to live. At Michael's funeral, my niece Katelynn played a beautiful video montage she had made about her dad's life. The video was set to favorite songs and began with baby pictures that morphed into toddler pictures and so on. Next came the pictures of Michael with my sister Christina and then him with his children and his friends. It's incredible to watch someone's entire life play out so quickly and if it is someone who passed early, it's bittersweet to see it cut short. As we were driving away from that funeral Dave was deep in thought . . . you'll remember that funerals are still relatively unusual for him.

He finally told me what was on his mind when we parked in front of where we were staying later that night.

"I can't stop thinking about Michael's video," he told me.

"I know, me either. It's so sad that there are no more pictures after those."

He nodded absently. "Yes, it is sad. But that's not what I keep thinking about. I keep thinking that we still have pictures left to take."

"What do you mean?"

"I mean that someday at my funeral or your funeral someone is going to make us a video like that, right?"

"I'm sure they will."

"And in it they'll choose the best pictures, the ones that represent who we are and the kind of life we lived, right?"

"Of course."

"Well, I want to live the kind of life that's worthy of the memorial video. I want to make sure I don't forget that there are people who don't get to take pictures anymore. I better not waste the opportunity."

DON'T WASTE THIS OPPORTUNITY.

THIS LIFE YOU'RE LIVING IS A WILDLY PRECIOUS GIFT THAT MOST PEOPLE TAKE FOR GRANTED. DON'T TAKE IT FOR GRANTED.

LIVE INTO EVERY INCH OF IT.

LIVE IT BOLDLY AND WITH COURAGE.

LIVE IT HOPEFULLY AND WITH KINDNESS.

LIVE IT AS YOURSELF.

LIVE IT FOR YOURSELF.

LIVE IT FOR THOSE WHO CAN'T.

LIVE IT FOR THOSE WHO WALK BESIDE YOU.

LIVE IT FOR THOSE WHO CAME BEFORE, THOSE WHO'VE PASSED ON, AND THOSE WHO WILL CARRY YOUR LEGACY FORWARD LONG AFTER YOU'RE GONE.

PLEASE, LIVE THIS BEAUTIFUL, HARD, WONDERFUL LIFE— and since you will live it, as you were always meant to do, resolve to live it well.

## ACKNOWLEDGMENTS

First and foremost, I must thank my editor Carrie Thornton for going above and beyond to help me bring this book into the world. Very few editors would be okay pushing away the book we were nearing the finish line on in order to take on a project like this, *inside of quarantine and a pandemic* and get it into the world on the tightest turnaround of all time. I sort of can't believe we actually pulled it off but I do believe there's no way I would have made it to print without your extreme hand-holding during this process.

Shout-out as always to my agent and friend Kevan Lyon who has been my champion since long before anyone knew my name or cared about what I was writing.

Special thank-you to the entire team at Dey Street: Liate Stehlik, Benjamin Steinberg, Heidi Richter, Kendra

Newton, Peter Kispert, Andrea Molitor, Pam Barricklow, Renata De Oliveira, Andy LeCount, Christine Edwards, and Josh Marwell. If creating this book on the fly, in a matter of weeks, threw any of you off, I was never aware of it. You are consummate professionals.

Honorable mention to my assistant, Ali Mudano, for having a pie thrown in her face again and again when we were testing ideas for the cover of this book. Thanks, Al, for taking one for the team, I pray the smell of whipped cream has finally washed out of your hair.

Thanks too to everyone else who helped make the cover happen: Vanessa Todd for the photos, Brad Chandler for the muscle, Katelynn Neeley for thousands of cans of whipped cream and shaving foam, and as always, my girl Sami Cromelin for the cover and jacket design.

Last but definitely not least, I want to thank my children: Jackson, Sawyer, Ford, and Noah. You are the best part of my life and I'm so lucky to be your mom.

## ABOUT THE AUTHOR

**RACHEL HOLLIS** laid the foundation for her lifestyle brand and media company with the same unfiltered honesty and staunch inclusivity that made her a two-time #1 *New York Times* bestselling author. Hollis connects with a highly engaged and growing global audience who treasure her transparency and optimism. She is one of the most sought-after motivational speakers, plays host to one of today's top business podcasts, and is a proud working mama of four who uses her platform to empower and embolden women around the world. Rachel calls Texas home; more specifically, the Hill Country just outside of Austin.

readytorise.com    @msrachelhollis

# NOTES

# NOTES

# NOTES

NOTES